Finding the Joy in Today

Finding the Joy in Today

*Practical Readings for Living
with Chronic Illness*

SEFRA KOBRIN PITZELE

Hazelden
Center City, Minnesota 55012-0176

1-800-328-0094
1-651-213-4590
www.hazelden.org

First published by Hazelden, April 1988

Library of Congress Cataloging-in-Publication Data

Pitzele, Sefra, 1942–
   [One more day]
   Finding the joy in today : practical readings for living with
chronic illness / Sefra Kobrin Pitzele.
        p.   cm.
   Originally published: One more day, c1988.
   Includes index.
   ISBN 1-56838-348-7
   1. Chronically ill Prayer-books and devotions—English.
2. Devotional calendars. I. Title.
BV4910.P57   1999
242'.4—dc21   99-37665
                                                   CIP

Cover design by David Spohn
Interior design by Donna Burch
Typesetting by Stanton Publication Services, Inc.

NOTE TO THE READER

While living with a chronic health condition can be difficult, it is not impossible. When you search for growth and joy in life, an ongoing health condition can provide a positive life force. When you set new personal goals—ones that you can reach—I pray you will find your inner strength by believing in yourself and finding and serving your source of Higher Power.

Marvelous opportunities for growth and joy await us—through doors we can open and pass through. Lean into your life and learn to be gentler and kinder to yourself.

SEFRA KOBRIN PITZELE

INTRODUCTION

As the new millennium approaches, we find that one out of three people have ongoing—or chronic—illness to deal with every day. This represents a huge number of people who may have difficulty embracing joy in their lives. This book is written to help you take each day in small, successful bites. It is hoped you will learn to see the joy each day can provide, in spite of your chronic health problems. I hope this book will help fulfill your need for connection.

Every day make a special effort to renew your spirit—your sense of attachment to nature and to the greater world around you. Do this by taking a moment to hear a child laugh, to listen to birds sing, or to reach out with a friendly smile or hug.

When I wrote my first book, *We Are Not Alone: Learning to Live with Chronic Illness,* I was new at being chronically ill. I have learned that it is in moving out of yourself to reach another that renews one's spirit. Life can be so wonderful that we must not waste a single day. Renew your spirit every day. I pray, for you, joy-filled days.

～ JANUARY 1 ～

*The beginning is the most important part
of the work.*
—Plato

On occasion we feel a bit sad as we ready ourselves for bed, knowing that our bedtime routine marks the end of another day. We may experience a slight sense of loss—time lost, opportunities lost, a piece of life gone forever. Or we may be filled with regret over words uttered harshly.

We can put this back into perspective with the realization that the nicest part about going to bed at night is knowing the daylight will come in the morning. We can't erase today's mistakes, but we can leave them with the day now past. We can set our sights on tomorrow. The day we awaken to will hold a golden opportunity— to make amends, to make changes, to use our time well, to start the rest of our lives anew.

*My life is made of some endings and many beginnings.
I can choose to end an unproductive pattern
by seeing it as a chance to begin.*

⌒ JANUARY 2 ⌒

Our share of night to bear,
Our share of morning . . .
—EMILY DICKINSON

We pray for one more day. One more week. Just until the next marker of time or the next major event occurs. "Just let me live until spring," we pray, "until my newest grandchild is born . . . until my next birthday." We pray and may not even recognize these silent, secret pleas as being prayers. It's human nature to ask for a little more time. Most of us feel as though we have not completed our role on earth.

Time, however, is gradually becoming more of a friend than an enemy. We have today, which is all that anyone—healthy or chronically ill—really ever has. No one has an iron-clad promise of weeks, months, or years. Our acceptance of life's unpredictability frees us of our preoccupation with *more* time and allows us to use *this* time—today.

Life is now— today— and I value it by living fully.

⸺ JANUARY 3 ⸺

Laugh at yourself first, before anybody else can.
—ELSA MAXWELL

A sense of humor is an essential living tool. Unfortunately, it is most difficult to keep a sense of humor when we're under stress, and that's the time we need it most. In the face of a crisis, we may have found it easier to be dour and nasty, even if we knew, deep in our hearts, that such an attitude was not in our best interests.

Ironically, our medical problems have helped many of us cultivate a humorous attitude toward life. Making the choice between bitterness and acceptance is easier when we take ourselves less seriously. Seeing the funny side of life helps us deal with the most difficult situations life has to offer. Humor cleanses us through spontaneous laughter. It draws others to us and bonds us.

I choose to see humor and lightness in my life.
I will allow this attitude to brighten my life
and that of those around me.

⌒ JANUARY 4 ⌒

Time is a dressmaker specializing in alterations.
— FAITH BALDWIN

Each stage of life brings its own gifts. Every age gives us a chance to examine where we are right now. When we were young, many of us insisted that we could change the world. We even thought we could change people. The next stage in life may have given us the gift of seeing that we could only change ourselves.

Whatever stage we are in right now is the perfect place to reassess our priorities again. It has become obvious to us by now which things we cannot change, and we are busily accepting that truth.

Time itself alters us and our expectations. The time we have lived has already created change, and the passing of time will create more. The alterations we make today can help us accept this stage in life as being the best place to be.

*Now is the time to alter my expectations of myself,
to tailor them to my current needs.*

We are never as fortunate or
as unfortunate as we suppose.
— LA ROUCHEFOUCAULD

Pain, especially continual pain, is very draining and is often one of the largest problems associated with chronic illness. In the beginning we may have reacted to our pain with anger or whining and, in doing so, came to see ourselves as victims or martyrs. That self-image made us feel helpless, powerless.

Now, we're better able to understand pain, not as a curse thrust upon us, but as our bodies' normal function. Pain is a signal and sometimes a warning. But pain can assist us now in better management of our illnesses by helping us regain some of our personal power and inner strength. Methods such as relaxation therapy, biofeedback, and self-hypnosis can all work on different levels to control our pain. Appropriate exercise can also be an excellent method of pain control.

I will explore ways to deal with my pain.

∼ JANUARY 6 ∼

A little learning is a dang'rous thing.
—ALEXANDER POPE

Since childhood we've been told that education is the key to success, to happiness, to almost all good things in life. We gradually gain knowledge as we go through school and continue through life, and at each plateau we feel more confident. But a crisis may undermine that confidence. Problems within our families, such as alcohol or other drug abuse or a chronic illness, can sharply point out how little we really know. Our reactions differ—some of us dive into a frenzy of denial and activity, while others are immobilized by fear and uncertainty.

But then we remember: Learning is the key; we don't have to know instinctively what to do. We can turn to others who have greater knowledge. Organizations are there to give us well-qualified assistance. We want and need to learn the truth.

*I don't have to have all the answers,
just the right questions.*

⌐ JANUARY 7 ⌐

All human wisdom is summed up in two words:
wait and hope.
—ALEXANDRE DUMAS

When we were children, the only waiting and hoping we did was short-term. We waited for the holidays. We hoped our parents wouldn't find out we got the carpet dirty.

Once a chronic medical problem is diagnosed, we become masters at the art of waiting and hoping. Waiting to see if the new medication helps. Hoping for a remission or cure.

We learn that in order to adjust we must help ourselves. One way we can help ourselves is to get in touch with one of the many self-help groups. These groups can offer us a sense of continuity, of inner strength, of hope for better times again. With deepened faith in ourselves and in our abilities, we discover a sense of inner peace.

Hope renews me and lets me face each day
with the best possible attitude.

⌐ JANUARY 8 ⌐

Along with success comes a reputation for wisdom.
— EURIPIDES

Our definition of success varies as we move through stages of life. While we once may have dreamed of a large lake home and a large salary, we may have settled for a modest home and salary. As we reevaluate our goals, we become aware that we have succeeded in our own way.

Success, for us, might mean we have many friends. Or that our children have become worthwhile citizens. We may feel successful largely because we have learned to accept ourselves—the total package of strengths and weaknesses. We set and reset our own goals throughout a lifetime, and our successes are measured, not by specific deeds or accumulations of cash, but by how well we set our goals and how faithful we are to them.

I'll look again at my values and goals
to be sure they leave me room for success.

⌐ JANUARY 9 ⌐

Every baby born into the world is
a finer one than the last.
— CHARLES DICKENS

Place a newborn infant in any adult's arms, and that adult will turn all attention to the tiny new life. Most of us feel overwhelmed with the miracle of birth and the beauty contained within that tiny body. To hold an infant is to feel perpetuity and an incredible sense of joy. In the infant, we see a projection of life and the full scope of life's possibilities.

Long ago, others marveled at the fragility and wonder of life as we were placed as babes in their arms. Now we recognize we all had the same beginnings; we all had time before us. We still have time, and it is still full of possibilities.

I marvel at the gift of life and all that lies before me.

∽ JANUARY 10 ∽

*In loving myself I gain the power of identity that
is necessary before love for others is possible.*
—David G. Jones

Throughout our lives, we may have loved and cared for other people more than we did for ourselves. Some of us were raised to feel that self-love meant selfish. And some of us had trouble finding anything in ourselves that we could love.

Learning to love ourselves is not easy, especially if our lives are not going the way we had hoped. And those of us who had expected greater personal growth are often unable to take pride in what progress we've made. If we hoped for perfection, we were bound to be disappointed.

Now, we're more likely to see self-love as meaning self-acceptance. We simply offer ourselves what we've so freely offered others—love, care, and a second chance.

*I am a worthy person,
deserving of love and forgiveness.*

⌐ JANUARY 11 ⌐

Always do one thing less than you think you can do.
— BERNARD BARUCH

Without even realizing it, we all have developed differ-ent levels of expertise. Too often, however, our knowl-edge of ourselves and of our physical capabilities is what we know the least of. The true measure of knowing our-selves, regardless of how capable we seem to be, is to stop the activity before we get too exhausted, before we have too much pain—before we cause an accident.

Understanding one's own body has become a pri-mary concern for many of us because now we realize that how we "used to" function doesn't matter anymore. What does matter is how our bodies function right now, and we learn to structure our goals and expectations around those limitations.

*I am learning, finally, how to recognize
and heed my own body's warning signals.*

～ JANUARY 12 ～

It's a fine thing to rise above pride,
but you must have pride in order to do so.
— GEORGE BERNANOS

We are entitled to feel proud of our accomplishments. Pride is an essential ingredient in the recipe of life, and it comes from an inner sense of well-being, from knowing we have done the best we could under difficult conditions.

When our day's plans are upset by the unexpected, we may struggle with maintaining our pride. We may have been completely independent but now have to rely on others. Or we may have had little pain before and are now overwhelmed by it. Increasingly, we see that we need to find a solution to these new problems or to adjust to those which have none. Solutions and adjustments may be difficult, but we are incorporating them into our lives. We are entitled to feel proud.

Pride is mine as I adjust to my new problems.

~ JANUARY 13 ~

We cannot live, sorrow or die for somebody else. . . .
— EDWARD DAHLBERG

Our need to protect a sick child becomes frustration as we can do so little to protect the child from pain. When we become ill, our families and friends sometimes make awkward efforts to help protect us. They may try to make us laugh by telling jokes or recounting funny moments we've shared with them. Or these people might become overly helpful, trying to save us some steps or inconvenience.

We understand their need to help us; all of us want to comfort and protect our loved ones as we would a child. However, we are not children, and the maturity we've gained has reversed the roles we play with our families and friends. We can comfort and protect them by laughing with them and by letting them help us, and this becomes a two-way expression of love.

Today, I will allow others to express their love for me.

⸺ JANUARY 14 ⸺

Ill health of body or of mind is defeat.
Health alone is victory. Let all men, if they can
manage it, contrive to be healthy.
— THOMAS CARLYLE

This message, on the surface, could be upsetting to people who are chronically ill. Can we be sick and healthy at the same time? We learn that we can. Even if we have an ongoing health need, we can still create a new frame of reference that allows us to be as healthy as we can. Rather than letting our problems run us into the ground, we can make the opposite choice.

We can choose balance in our lives by deciding to put the problem in its place as only one facet of our lives. At the moment we decide, at the moment we make a conscious decision to be a fighter, we will be striving toward wellness once again.

By constructively choosing to keep a
strong attitude emotionally and physically,
I will be on the road to balanced health.

The person who tries to live alone will not
succeed as a human being.
—PEARL S. BUCK

We all enjoy going out to dinner or to a movie. Some of us who are not well, however, choose to become stay-at-homes. Our reasons are many, and one big reason is we don't want to be stared at or singled out as different. But, in hiding from the stares, we also hide from ourselves.

We don't want to put ourselves on the line, but we must if we are to become "public" once again. It may mean using a cane or a brace; it may mean utilizing some of the fine adaptive-living aids invented to help us. It's a hard decision, but not as hard as being alone and staying at home.

It takes tremendous inner strength to venture from
the protective cocoon of my home. I have the same
inner strength as always, and I can use
it to survive tough times.

The future is an opaque mirror. Anyone who looks into it sees nothing but the dim outlines of an old and worried face.
—JIM BISHOP

When we are young, our mirrors reflect our outer appearance. Later, mirrors seem to reflect also the inward self. Worry and joy can etch themselves into our facial expressions; anger or love can gaze out from our eyes. If we have refused to forgive, our bitterness stares back at us. If we have chosen to isolate ourselves, our loneliness is there. But if our choices have been openness, humor, and understanding, all of these clearly shine out for all to see.

Each day, without realizing it, we are making choices for behaviors and thoughts that will help create either a serene and joyful face or an old and worried one. The choice is ours.

Today, I choose healthy looks, actions, and feelings.

⌐ JANUARY 17 ⌐

Probably no one alive hasn't at one time or
another brooded over the possibility of going back
to an earlier, ideal age in his existence and
living a different kind of life.
—HAL BOYLE

If we could go back to a more perfect, idyllic life, what section of life would we choose? As we daydream about the wonderful "yesterdays" in our lives, little do we realize that even though our health and life circumstances may have changed somewhat, we could, right at this very moment, be creating the memories upon which we will look back fondly.

We make our own good times and our own good memories. We can't ever go backward—but we do still have the ability and capacity to move forward.

I am aware that it's up to me to create all my
future memories. I can take from life only as
much as I am willing to put into it.

~ JANUARY 18 ~

Life's a pretty precious and wonderful thing.
You can't sit down and let it lap around you . . .
you have to plunge into it, you have to dive through it.
—KYLE CRICHTON

Life isn't always carefree. Especially when we are suffering pain and discomfort, we may tend to back away from the mainstream. We're just not sure how to behave in the face of new problems. We become confused about what is expected of us and what we expect from others. Uncertain of what to do, we may be content for a while to let life lap around us.

We find, however hard the lesson, that in order to be a participant, to get into the swing of things, we must dive back into life. No one is going to take care of all our needs. We are responsible for our actions.

I have been confused how to continue living
my life. Now I understand that I must
plunge in again and get going.

～ JANUARY 19 ～

Wisdom is knowing when you can't be wise.
— PAUL ENGLE

Whenever we previously thought of wisdom, we may have imagined either a venerated sage or a beloved grandparent. Or we may have thought of formal schooling and college degrees.

We remember wisdom learned from our parents. We remember conveying similar ideas to our children. How many of us really remember the first time we had to answer, "I don't know"? And what about the moment when it finally occurred to us that there are certain skills that we will never be able to develop?

Understanding comes when we expand ourselves to our fullest capacities and accept ourselves just as we are. Then and only then are we wise.

*The more comfortable I become with my limitations,
the more I can grow.*

～ JANUARY 20 ～

Life is full of internal dramas . . .
played to an audience of one.
—ANTHONY POWELL

Our lives are filled with dramas. Some of them we were able to talk about to similarly involved people, and some, we found, had to remain private.

Health changes can create hundreds of new dramas. In the beginning, far too many of us made the mistake of telling our experiences to anyone who asked. We talked too often, too long, and too much.

We are learning that gentle lesson of who, when, and how much to tell—selectivity. We discover that no one really wants to be always involved in our dramas, in each tiny success or failure. We can keep our own counsel and give ourselves private praise.

I can choose when— and when not—
to share some of the dramas in my life.

Historic continuity with the past is not a duty,
it is a necessity.
—OLIVER WENDELL HOLMES

Our personal histories mark the pathways of life. Our having lived and loved and worked makes a difference in thousands of ways. This impact on life is a history and heritage for our loved ones and for ourselves. What memories have we created for those we love? Perhaps quilts that will be treasured as family heirlooms. A family farm or profession. But what else?

Even more important than heirlooms and family jobs are loving memories and personal histories. Recorded histories, especially anecdotal, can be written or tape recorded. Pictures can be taken, and older photos can be labeled for the generations to come. What will we leave when we die? Communication, tradition, and the ability to love unconditionally.

This small but important moment is a good time
to record my journey thus far and to affirm
my sense of continuity.

~ JANUARY 22 ~

To live happily is an inward power of the soul.
— MARCUS AURELIUS

While we were still very healthy, we may not have realized how much we depended on others for our physical and emotional well-being. Perhaps we rarely turned toward our own strength or to a Power greater than ourselves. Because we had depended so little on ourselves, we may have, at first, felt defeated.

Ironically, we've become strengthened by illness. Soul searching and taking personal inventory are tools we use to discover the mental and spiritual reserves that were always available to us but little used.

The love and support of others are still important to us, but now we have a greater sense of balance that strengthens us and our relationships.

My inner spiritual messages transcend my need to depend on others. This strengthens me, my faith, and all the people touched by my life.

Those wrinkles are the map of my life. . . .
They're battle scars.
—ETTA FURLOW

One woman calls her wrinkles a patina that glows only with age. When first we notice tiny wrinkles—crow's-feet or smile lines—we may lament our loss of youth.

Naturally, our faces change as we age. Our life experiences, both joy and pain, etch themselves on our faces as surely as they mold our minds and spirits. Our bodies may begin to change as well. Previously nimble fingers may stiffen; backaches and a slowed pace may become the norm.

Skin is but a wrapping for the inner soul, and the soul's enjoyment of life is not diminished by its wrapping. Our spirits never grow old. Our belief in the beauty and joy of life is renewed with each season. And we remain strong.

My body will change as the years go by, but I
will stay aware of my spirit and faith. This keeps
me emotionally vibrant.

~ JANUARY 24 ~

The type of hugging I recommend is the bear hug.
Use both arms, face your partner and
perform a full embrace.
—DAVID BRESLER

We all need physical contact. And this contact does more than put us in touch with other people; it reminds us of our human need to love as well as to be loved.

Some of us may have a sense of aloneness, regardless of how many or few people surround us. If we live alone, it can be most difficult to get our daily ration of hugging and touching. Perhaps we need to consider buying a pet. A bird, a cat, a dog will offer affection all the time. All they require is a good, loving home. Or perhaps we need to think about the contact we have with others. Our expressions of love bring us the un-expected bonus of physical well-being.

I need to love and be loved. I will share my caring
nature more freely with other living creatures.

*Self-understanding rather than self-condemnation
is the way to inner peace and mature conscience.*
—Joshua Loth Liebman

We can be committees of one, single-handedly striving to show others, by example, that having a chronic medical problem need not keep us out of the mainstream of life. Our health difficulties may heighten our awareness of the value of life, of other people, and of ourselves.

We can hold our heads up high and go out in public. In this way, we refuse to let our diminished health subdue us. By being comfortable with ourselves, smiling at passers-by, and not complaining, we can create an aura of strength and self-assurance. Doing this can challenge and inspire others, and—more important—it can do the same for us.

*It's difficult sometimes to leave the security of my home.
The more I understand my fears, the easier it is
to go out among other people.*

In human relationships, closeness and warmth
only occur when we ask about one another . . .
when we seek to know how we can help one another.
Until we ask, we will never know.
—BERNARD S. RASKAS

Who are our close friends? We should cherish friendships and protect them as vigorously as we would a newborn infant.

When a friend comes to us needing our help, we are forced into making a decision. One choice—abandonment—means we lose a friend. The other option means that the question "What can I do to help you?" is no longer rhetorical; it is a commitment to helpfulness. We may even have to put ourselves at risk, especially emotionally, but we can be a friend who stays around when a crisis occurs.

I honor my close friendships. I am not someone who
takes and doesn't give personally. I can help others.

The ancient sage, who concocted the maxim,
"Know thyself," might have added, "Don't tell anyone!"
—H. F. HEINRICHS

All too often people hide from their own feelings and from the reality of chronic illness. We may reason that if we ignore it long enough, it will go away. Of course, this does not happen, and slowly we gain the knowledge of what our illness is and how we can best live with the changes it creates.

Perhaps we cannot change the course of a chronic illness or medical condition, but we can, and certainly should, change how we react. Bitterness only encourages the company of those who are also bitter. Acceptance, openness, and serenity will attract others who share our willingness to change and grow.

Today, I will be open and honest with myself as I move back into the path of life with an illness at my side.

⌇ JANUARY 28 ⌇

Love received and love given
comprise the best form of therapy.
—GORDON W. ALLPORT

Many of us with health problems are—by choice or by
necessity—alone, and we may sometimes feel uneasy in
a world geared for couples and families. Everywhere
there seems to be yet another couple—on a park bench,
strolling on the sidewalk, and on television. This is
especially painful if we had, at one time in our lives, a
happy, long-term relationship.

Now, we are finding a more complete and less re-
strictive sense of companionship and are still maintaining our independence. Romantic love is not the only
basis for trust and friendship. A friend we can trust may
also become a confidant, a strong emotional supporter,
and an all-around booster. We may be alone, but we realize that we need not be lonely.

I am lucky to have one close friend. I am blessed
when I have several. I am no longer alone.

～ JANUARY 29 ～

There is one thing a man cannot change— his parents.
—DAVID BEN-GURION

Sometimes we carry anger for too long and may blame others for our problems. It's time to let go if we have been harboring anger toward our parents or other adults. In our memory, in our perception, they may have harmed us. Regardless of what happened, whether it was imagined or real, we need to let it go.

Unknowingly, we may have developed an attachment to this anger toward our parents, and it may take a professional therapist or a support group to help us break the dependency. We can take responsibility for ourselves and our own behaviors. By no longer blaming our inappropriate actions on anyone else, we can free ourselves of one unhealthy aspect of our lives.

I am attempting to own my life and not see it as an extension of others. Today, I can take responsibility for myself and my actions.

⤸ JANUARY 30 ⤹

*If you make friends with yourself
you will never be alone.*
—MAXWELL MALTZ

Sometimes, we frantically adopt other people's problems to avoid confronting our own. Hiding from ourselves and our problems solves nothing. Yet some of us are so frightened by the challenge life has thrown before us that we are reluctant to confront it head-on.

Most important is being able to face ourselves, especially when we are alone. We can't always hide in the hustle and bustle of a crowd. But we can find a comfort level within ourselves, regardless of what we face. Then, when our spirituality is deepened and we understand our own struggles—and only then—can we assist, support, and share with others.

*My awareness of myself has been enhanced
by my new life circumstances. The deeper I dig,
the more soul I find. The more soul I find,
the more I can share myself.*

I recommend you to take care of the minutes,
for the hours will take care of themselves.
—LORD CHESTERFIELD

When a lifelong job is over, when a health problem occurs or mobility becomes impaired, when family moves away, the days may become long and lonely. Then, more than ever, it's important that we take care of our own needs. Some needs may be immediate, for we have far more time than we know how to fill. We may look toward the future, afraid of all the time that must be filled.

This is a perfect time to reach out into the community, to begin volunteer work. There are always people who need us, and by offering our help we will be helping ourselves as well. Each day is new and has new possibilities.

I refuse to worry about the future or the past.
Instead, I'll try to make a difference today.

⟶ FEBRUARY 1 ⟵

Snow endures but for a season,
and joy comes with the morning.
—MARCUS AURELIUS

We are a nation that sometimes sells out for short-term goals and short-term gratification. We may overuse credit cards. At times we live on impulse and buy on impulse. Gone is the long-term planning our parents tried to teach us as children. Gone is learning to wait.

Now we have no choice. Life's circumstances, especially illness, force us to wait whether or not we want to. True, we live with pain and annoyance, but once again, quite accidentally, we begin to know the joy that comes from waiting and from savoring any small victory.

Patience is a virtue I am once again cultivating.
Life's circumstances have taught me the
importance of finding the joy in each day.

～ FEBRUARY 2 ～

Every calamity is a spur and valuable hint.
— RALPH WALDO EMERSON

Events that felt like calamities when we were young have little importance as we get older. Experiences we had labeled "disastrous"—not having a date for the prom or failing a math test—now are unimportant or possibly even amusing.

Understanding that many events have only brief importance can help us view current problems more realistically. Not having enough money at the end of the month, family disagreements, and even a flare-up or worsening of a chronic illness are all very important, and they require our attention or adjustment. But we deal with these problems better because we've learned that few, if any, problems are really "disastrous." They're inconvenient or even painful, but our lives can accommodate them. We go on.

*I won't see calamities in today's problems
and inconveniences.*

⌣ FEBRUARY 3 ⌣

Every new adjustment is a crisis in self-esteem. . . .
—ERIC HOFFER

Wouldn't it be nice if our self-esteem could be as firmly rooted as our personalities seem to have been by the time we started school? Unfortunately that's not often the case. Self-esteem is very delicate and remains subject to the whims of all external circumstances including how people act toward us and how we react, in turn, to them.

An illness that changes how we look or how we think of ourselves can be continually demanding. Fighting the battle to maintain a good self-image requires adjustments of our time and goals. Making these adjustments turns our disappointments into chances for success.

I must continue to work on being a whole person
and try to develop all my facets —
spiritual, emotional, and physical.

～ FEBRUARY 4 ～

*A simple grateful thought raised to heaven
is the most perfect prayer.*
—GOTTHOLD EPHRAIM LESSING

Can we picture ourselves as small children, bouncing back out of bed to add just one more, "and also bless my teddy bear, and my . . . "? Most of us prayed because that's what we were taught to do. We didn't understand many of the reasons, but it felt good and made us feel safe too.

We form new habits as grown-ups. Perhaps prayer isn't part of our day anymore. We may start to pray only when we need to ask for something. It is within our reach to develop the habit of prayer once again. There may be comfort in the habit of giving thanks every day . . . for what good health we do enjoy . . . for the beauty of nature . . . for our families and friends.

*I will use prayer as one of the ways I can
express myself and live a fulfilling life.*

⌒ FEBRUARY 5 ⌒

We have seen better days.
— SHAKESPEARE

It is quite difficult to define some of the components that help create what we interpret as a good day. A general sense of well-being prevails, and we have a tendency to look at the world through rose-colored glasses. Everything seems to go just right.

It is not the least bit hard, however, to define a bad day. Nothing happens according to plan. We feel out of sorts, not particularly well. With the advent of health changes, we can inadvertently allow many days to become bad ones.

The only way we can stop having negative experiences is to change our expectations of what constitutes a good day. We don't have to lower our expectations, just make them more realistic for the situation at hand. We will then find that most of our days can be good ones.

*My life is and will always be a mixture of good
and bad days. I can influence my interactions
and thereby influence the color of my days.*

Grow old along with me! The best is yet to be.
—ROBERT BROWNING

We all have been to beautiful weddings. A young couple's love is so obvious. They have so much to look forward to, so much living is still ahead.

We understand more and more that now is the best time of our lives. Whether we are having a cup of coffee with a friend or fishing on a quiet lake, these are the best times.

As we age and reach the later decades of our lives, we become aware, even more sharply, that surely these are the best times of our lives. We feel comfortable with ourselves and what we have, and with what we are still accomplishing. We don't set unreasonable goals anymore. And we are lucky, too, for we can blend all our previous years of experience into our daily lives.

I am comforted by knowing that every stage of my life presents me with new opportunities.

∼ FEBRUARY 7 ∼

Of all sad words of tongue or pen,
The saddest are these: It might have been.
—JOHN GREENLEAF WHITTIER

A story is told of a man leaning over his wife's casket. "I waited too long," he lamented to no one in particular. "Why didn't I tell her how much I loved her, how much I cherished our life together? I waited too long."

Like everyone else, we are guilty of procrastination. We tend to put off difficult decisions, such as ending a bad relationship or quitting a job or making amends with an old friend. Our procrastinations seem to protect us.

Now we understand that time is important too. The more we put something off, the less time we have for other more positive areas of life. Life gets easier when we don't procrastinate.

I can resolve many problems with direct actions.
I need not procrastinate anymore.

*Tragedy is an initiation not of human beings
but of action, life, happiness and unhappiness.*
—ARISTOTLE

Our response to tragedy can be rage, sorrow, or even horror. Those responses, as real as they are, are not as accurate as our optimism, for it is optimism—the belief that life will go smoothly—that gives the label "tragedy" to an event. We are surprised, we are shocked when our optimism is leveled by the unexpected.

A tragedy is an event, a time, a moment, and nothing more. People's lives are constantly seesawing between emotions and events. No one is always happy, placid, or tragic. In experiencing life to the fullest, we expose ourselves to all its facets. And that simple act makes us all uniquely human.

*I accept my life and the ups and downs
of my human experience.*

⚮ FEBRUARY 9 ⚮

A chronic illness invades life.
—KATHLEEN LEWIS

Chronic illness means permanently changing our mindset to realize we can move only forward from this point in our lives. Chronic illness means pushing back the "front tears" in our minds so we can expand the frontiers of our days. Being ill means sometimes laughing with tears trapped in our hearts, so we won't have to be singled out as different from others. Chronic illness is becoming used to how we look today, right now, and not wasting more time longing for lost yesterdays.

If we haven't realized it yet, we will need more emotional support than perhaps at any other time in our experience. Regardless of how strong and independent we may be, we need comfort and support from those who love us.

Longing for the "old days" and "old ways" won't bring them back. I am learning to accept changes. They are not imposing upon my life—they are my life.

∽ FEBRUARY 10 ∽

The best thinking has been done in solitude.
The worst has been done in turmoil.
—THOMAS EDISON

When the rush of a busy world becomes overwhelming, we can restore ourselves to peace and tranquility. When we feel battered by the stress of the day, it's time to take a few moments for relaxation. We need to steady ourselves; in fact, we owe it to ourselves.

Solitude, meditation, serenity—these can be ours if we settle in for a few moments of private time. Alone. Taking this time is not self-indulgent; it's self-care and simple to do. We can tune the radio to some beautiful, soft music and sit back with a cup of herbal tea. Taking slow breaths, we can allow our bodies to relax with the warmth of the tea, the beauty of the music, and the solitude of the moment.

I relish the gift of privacy and relaxation each day.

— FEBRUARY 11 —

You are responsible for your own life
and have a job to perform in your health care.
—NEIL A. FIORE

It's a real shock to find out that we have an ongoing medical problem. Lots of us may get quite angry and blame the doctor for the diagnosis. Or we may want to turn it all over to the professionals. But soon we begin to see that we are the primary ones responsible for ourselves. Eventually, we begin to give full cooperation to our doctors and therapists. We become equal members of our health-care team.

Adjustments are difficult in the best of circumstances, but with the help of those who love us, with the assistance of our doctors, and with our participation, we adjust to chronic illness. Then we can see our problems in their proper perspective and begin again to enjoy our lives.

In accepting changes in my life,
I find balance once again.

~ FEBRUARY 12 ~

I am where I am because I believe in life's possibilities.
—OPRAH WINFREY

During the years of our youth we were continually reminded, "You can do it. Just set a goal and then reach a little beyond it." Many of us were better at this as youngsters than we are as adults. We each have fought our own battles—to become educated or perhaps to achieve a promotion or new job. We tend to get a little shortsighted when a new variable enters the picture—a changing health pattern.

Too many of us back away, fearful that we'll have all we can do to just orchestrate our own health care. It's imperative that we continue to believe in ourselves as human beings with great potential—it matters less that we reach each goal. It matters most that we try.

*I am setting new goals that offer challenge
and the chance for success.*

Joy waits for no man.
— TANHUMA

Joyfulness is one of God's greatest gifts. Joy transcends all time and place. Joy causes unmeasurable and often indescribable feelings which we might have for only a fleeting moment. Joy is like opening a special present. It is a state of mind, a frame of reference for future memories.

While we may quite easily recognize the joy of watching an exquisite sunset, we forget too often that it is natural that its beauty changes, dims, and then disappears within moments. And this is true of many of our joy-filled experiences—they change, they dim, and often they disappear. Joy does not always stay with us, so we need to make the most of it when it is upon us—in a sunset, a child's hug, or a friend's offered hand.

To live life to the fullest, I am open to those special moments of joy, even if they don't last forever.

FEBRUARY 14

We don't love qualities, we love persons. . . .
— JACQUES MARITAIN

No matter what happens to us in our lifetime, regardless of whether we are rich or poor, strong or weak, ill or well, we always have room for love. Unqualified love and caring cost nothing. Despite our financial position, allowing ourselves to love, allowing ourselves to be loved strengthens and lends greater value to our lives.

In loving others and in being loved, we are reminded that people, not events or even characteristics, are the important elements of our lives. We don't look for perfection in our loved ones, and we're freed of the notion that we must earn another's love. Love balances our lives; it helps us keep sight of our values and priorities.

I will remember today that I love people for
themselves, not for their potential. The love
I receive is given just as freely.

∼ FEBRUARY 15 ∼

Reality is a staircase going neither up nor down,
we don't move, today is today, always is today.
—OCTAVIO PAZ

Reality is a harsh word and can invade our everyday lives. When we are struggling to cope with the physical changes that occur with long-term medical problems, reality becomes our constant companion. No longer can we deny anxiety or discomfort.

Our self-imposed rules might be the framework of our lives, but we can build a new structure which accepts illness as part of the reality of our lives. This new structure can have much more depth and greater dimension than the original, for we are older and wiser. Part of the framework that gives our days meaning is our love for friends and family and recognition of our spiritual capacity. These, too, become our new reality.

I no longer expect perfect health, but I can
minimize my complaining and maximize my efforts
to live a meaningful life.

Every soul is a melody which needs renewing.
—STEPHNE MELLARME

It may be difficult to admit how discordant our lives become at times—and even more difficult to restore a sense of peace. We may plunge into self-improvement programs with the idea that we, and we alone, can fix ourselves and ease our emotional pain. In doing this, we ignore the spiritual resources outside ourselves.

We better understand and accept our human flaws now and find it easier to ask God for help. Occasionally we may feel inadequate or angry or frightened. We question and doubt ourselves; we get lost in the maze of our own emotions. But we know these feelings are only temporary and that the calming spiritual tempo of our lives is briefly being drowned out by the emotions of the moment. It is comforting to know the melody is always there.

Today, I trust God to keep me in tune
with the peace within.

~ FEBRUARY 17 ~

*Grace is the absence of everything that indicates
pain or difficulty, hesitation or incongruity.*
—WILLIAM HAZLITT

It seems that, when we think our lives are back on course, another obstacle appears and we stumble. In the case of physical illness, symptoms or pains may worsen or new problems may crop up. Other circumstances can make our stress level rise as well, until it feels as though we just can't carry the burden anymore.

Adjustments can be very difficult. With new symptoms we may feel that illness is chipping away, one tiny piece at a time, at our independence. It's difficult to be gracious with so many complications going on. Yet this is the time to be gracious—to ourselves and to those around us.

*If I have ever needed to reach into my innermost
being to find peace and contentment, it is now.
I dislike what has happened to my body,
but I can continue to be a gracious person.*

Self-pity is our worst enemy and if we yield to it,
we can never do anything wise in this world.
—HELEN KELLER

Pity, either from ourselves or others, harms us. Yet, sometimes, we allow it to happen.

What we really need from others is empathy—for them to feel as if they were in our shoes. Pity can be a deep pit to fall into, and the climb back out is difficult. We can't begin to make the ascent until we are fully aware of why we have allowed pity and self-pity to prevail. Maybe feeling sorry for ourselves has been easier than encountering the frustration that may come when we make an effort.

The actions I take today will be based on
growth for myself and will help me avoid self-pity.

Arriving at one goal is the starting point to another.
—JOHN DEWEY

Accepting change in our lives is the basis of growth. Too often, we've seen change as threatening—familiar landmarks are razed, friends move away or die, we become ill.

Eventually, we come to see change in a different light. For good or bad, or whether we approve or don't approve, change will happen. The only thing we can control is our reaction to it. Change that is progress or growth, such as old landmarks disappearing and new ones being built or friends becoming involved in self-help groups, can be welcomed. Other changes that can't be greeted with enthusiasm—losing friends or becoming ill—can at least be seen as random, not personal, consequences of human life. With this frame of mind, we are able to accept the challenges demanded of us.

Changes in my life can encourage growth.

⟋ FEBRUARY 20 ⟍

This is a delicious evening,
when the whole body is one sense
and imbibes delight through every pore.
—HENRY DAVID THOREAU

We carry the memory of a soft spring rain within us even in a dry season. We remember the pungent fragrance of new-mown grass, the chirping of crickets, the singing of birds.

Such memories are important to us, but we're increasingly determined to also create new ones. It takes some planning on our part to get out, but we know the experience is worth the effort. Our mobility may be limited, or we might not be living in a place where we can commune with nature as easily as we did when we were younger. But we're creative and find the joy of outdoors on the stoop of our building or on a park bench. Zoos, nature preserves, and public parks give us areas for today's enjoyment and tomorrow's memories.

My illness imposes real limitations upon me;
I will not impose artificial ones upon myself.

～ FEBRUARY 21 ～

I will not keep myself from taking positive action.
—K. O'BRIEN

The inability to get going can sometimes plague us. Muscles that don't work properly or joints that won't bend can keep us from beginning the day as we once did, even if we have excellent intentions.

Excellent intentions only, however, get us nowhere unless we act upon them. What we need is that extra measure of strength, drawn from some inner resource that we hold in store only for days such as these. Often those sources spring from our intense belief that we will make it through these difficult times. Gradually we recognize that our actions and reactions are becoming more positive.

I try to reach a little bit further for the strength I need to fulfill my good intentions.

The soul would have no rainbow
Had the eyes no tears.
—JOHN VANCE CHENEY

That familiar tightening in the throat, the welling of tears behind the eyes, and deep emotional pain are all signs of an intense need to cry. Why do we try so hard to be "brave little soldiers" and not cry when our bodies are screaming for release?

If we hide behind false smiles and continue to keep the well of emotion untapped, eventually that well will go dry. Deprived of this natural outlet, our minds and bodies exhaust themselves as they battle tension and stress. We lose our ability to express ourselves emotionally. There may be no more opportunity for tears. Tears cleanse and allow other emotions to move in and take over until we need to cry again.

Crying releases me and gives me the freedom
to experience my full range of feelings.

Who can separate his faith from his actions,
or his belief from his occupations?
—KAHLIL GIBRAN

We may, at times, represent ourselves in an untrue fashion. This may happen when we are trying to impress someone who doesn't know us well. We may unconsciously try to imitate another person. Yet in doing so we are not being faithful to the gift of our own uniqueness.

Our need to "prove ourselves" diminishes only when self-esteem and self-awareness blossom. As we become more secure, we begin to honestly express ourselves and our faith. We no longer need heroes to worship; we can instead honor the gift of life.

I find comfort in the honest expression
of my beliefs and feelings.

The future is like heaven—
everyone exalts it but no one wants to go there now.
—JAMES BALDWIN

There are people called futurists who specialize in studying trends and attitudes and who then form theories as to what the future will hold. Having a reasoned opinion about future needs is important for business, education, and industry. It's probably not so important for us. We work harder to understand today and to discover what this day can hold for us.

We aren't scientists or researchers; we are more like explorers who face uncharted territory. Each morning we're unaware of all the events and surprises that lie ahead, but we are the only ones who can choose the direction this day will take. We don't want to and we don't need to worry about the future because right now we have this gift of time to use for ourselves and for those who are close to us.

I will glory in this day and fill it with living.

~ FEBRUARY 25 ~

He who attempts to resist the wave is swept away,
but he who bends before it abides.
—LEVITICUS

Just as water transforms the definition of the shoreline, so can our changing health patterns alter the boundaries of our days. What looked and felt normal before may be entirely alien now.

In various stages of life, we've repeatedly demonstrated our ability to adapt to new situations. Marriage, children, new jobs all call for personal change. Add to these everyday occurrences a chronic medical condition (physical or emotional) and we may feel we are drowning. Perhaps at these times we can disengage ourselves from the moment, reassess the past, and recall how well we've handled the changes life has demanded. We have been adaptable, and we can continue to be.

Creating a new pattern of living
is definitely within my reach.

I shall not pass this way again;
Then let me now relieve some pain,
Remove some barrier from the road,
Or brighten someone's heavy load.
— EVA ROSE YORK

Sometimes we help others through neighborhood cleanup committees, recycling stations, and paint-a-thons. Maybe we've volunteered through school or church or community organizations.

Illness has helped us better understand the relationship between those who help and those who need help. Loving help is not prompted by pity or superiority, but by empathy and shared humanness. Also, we've learned that no one is always the helper or always the one needing help. We are both. We are bonded to others through what we give—and what we receive.

I will show my love by helping
and being willing to be helped.

~ FEBRUARY 27 ~

Friendship needs no words—
it is solitude delivered from the anguish of loneliness.
—DAG HAMMARSKJÖLD

The meaning of *pregnant pause* is clear when we are with close friends. We feel no need to entertain them. There is comfort in the silence.

A friend knows almost intuitively when we have pain and when we do not. A friend lets us ramble on as we try to adjust to a changing lifestyle. We make judgments about how much to share. Even friends can be wearied by an endless litany of complaints. We trust our friends, but we also trust the comfort of silent understanding.

I am thankful for my friends with whom
I can share in words and in silence.

We all like to forgive, and we all love best not those who offend us least, not those who have done the most for us, but those who make it most easy for us to forgive them.
—SAMUEL BUTLER

None of us likes to harbor angry or bitter feelings toward another person. We know that friends may drift apart because of disagreements in which neither of us will bend or compromise.

More and more, we know what our values are and the importance of how we reflect those values. When a friendship is threatened by anger or misunderstanding, we're able to let our values guide us. We've been less willing to sacrifice our values to save a weak relationship. We've let go of some friends. If we've been stubborn or selfish, we're better able now to preserve the friendship by making amends.

I will nurture my friendships and myself by letting my principles guide my life.

There is no way to peace. Peace is the way.
—A. J. MUSTE

So often we look for easy answers and quick remedies. We want to reach our goals—now. Whatever we're looking for (peace, love, acceptance), we may be making the mistake of seeing these qualities as concrete, hold-in-my-hand goals.

Gradually, we're coming to the understanding that those qualities we seek are not destinations; they are paths and directions we can consciously take. We can't go out and find love, but we can choose to be loving. There is no path to peace or to acceptance or to understanding, but we can base our lives on these qualities, and by doing so we claim them.

What I seek may already be within my soul.

*Bitterness and anger seem to be very closely related
and are interchangeable words for the same emotion.*
— ROBERT LOVERING

Why me? We may rage with anger or disbelief when we finally realize we may never fully regain good health. In the beginning, while we are still getting used to our new situation, this happens to most of us. And then we ask, "Why me?"

Having a chronic medical condition is not as likely to create bitterness as much as making poor choices about how to respond to it. If we choose loneliness or a lifestyle that allows no room for laughter, we choose bitterness.

By making healthier choices, we affirm our belief in ourselves, in the possibilities life has to offer. We feel more loving toward the people around us and, in turn, are more loving toward ourselves.

*I can learn to balance my negative feelings
with contentment and happiness.
I can gain strength from my illness.*

People, by and large, will relate to the image you project. . . . If you project the image of a sick, dependent person, that's how you'll be treated.
— CHYATTE

Accepting chronic illness is not easy. Our whole lives are different. We can't do all the things we used to do. We may feel changed and be afraid of the changes our illnesses will bring. But as we learn to project a strong, positive image, we feel better about ourselves.

For the benefit of ourselves, we must act as if we are doing all right. When we act as if we are strong, our new behavior can become a new habit, and that habit can actually develop greater emotional strength within us. We can put illness into perspective as being just one of the changes that occur during a lifetime.

Today, I will allow myself the right to change. I can survive my health change and live a worthwhile life.

~ MARCH 4 ~

Whatever limits us, we call fate.
— RALPH WALDO EMERSON

We like to plan ahead, but we cannot plan for the ravages of chronic illness. No one expects to travel down the winding road of an unbidden, unwanted trip. Unused to the whims of a chronic illness, we may at first try to chart, plan, and control its course. We may dwell too much on our medical conditions.

We cannot change the course of illness, but we can influence its twists and turns by keeping a positive frame of mind. Rather than being obsessed with how our medical conditions are affecting us, we can focus on the many things we can still do. Can we enjoy a sunset? Watch a child smile? Can we listen to music or pursue a handcraft? Our angry, dour thoughts can be replaced so easily with pleasant dreams, fond memories, and hope for the future.

I am feeling comfortable once again
as I finally realize that I can still make choices
in how I want to live my life.

～ MARCH 5 ～

*Our sweetest songs are those
that tell of saddest thoughts.*
— PERCY BYSSHE SHELLEY

Our inner messages are much like tuning a radio; we choose what we want to hear. With a turn of the radio dial, the music changes from mellow and happy to sad and lonely and back again.

The inner messages we choose to hear may fill our days with memories that are difficult to bear. But we can tune our minds to more positive thoughts by noticing the beauty of our surroundings, by focusing on more pluses and on fewer minuses. We can, willingly, switch our minds to thoughts that are better for us and for our health.

Why should we listen to the sad, lonely sounds when we have other choices? We can choose a daily program to suit our goals and needs, one that enhances desires and improves general well-being.

*Today, I will turn my personal dial
to more positive messages.*

∼ MARCH 6 ∼

The unfortunate thing about this world is that good habits are so much easier to give up than bad ones.
— SOMERSET MAUGHAM

Old habits often die hard, especially bad ones. We may need to be tactfully silent when we become irritated with the behavior or habits of our loved ones. It may seem at times as though everyone around us is either nail biting, smoking, cussing, or overeating. When illness enters the scene, or any other stressor for that matter, bad habits tend to resurface. We may be less tolerant of others' faults and even of their good health.

It's hard to put away old habits, especially the old pattern of being critical, but we can learn to let go. Even with extra stress in our lives we can begin to work on developing new habits. We can learn to recognize the growth we've achieved and to feel proud.

I can begin today to develop strong new habits and to hold on to my old strong habits.

～ MARCH 7 ～

Life, if you will, is a work of art,
and if we have paid loving attention to its details,
we will be able to take pride in the finished product.
—HAROLD KUSHNER

Without even realizing it, we often do things that are good for us and make us happy. We do something that creates well-being, and we have a successful day. When we pay attention to actions that create well-being, we can have a successful week. Taking good care of our homes makes us feel proud and so does helping a fellow human being in need. Making volunteer work a part of how we live, showing kindness to others and ourselves, reaching out—all these choices enhance our well-being.

When we pay attention to those around us, a transformation occurs within our spiritual selves. Then we shall have given ourselves the gift of a meaningful life.

I will pay loving attention to the details of my day.

We cannot learn without pain.
— ARISTOTLE

It is said that pain and experience are life's two greatest teachers. What good would it be if we felt pain each day but never learned from it? And what good would it be if we coasted through life without experiencing joy along with sorrow?

There can be no depth of personality or depth of character if our lives have been perfect. Experience etches our hearts and souls, gives us depth, and deepens the horizon of our days. No individual has lived a life completely without pain, without sorrow. We can move beyond our pain and sorrow to grow in new directions.

I can accept the lessons I am learning of tolerance to living a less-than-perfect life. These lessons help me grow.

*Don't waste today regretting yesterday
instead of making a memory for tomorrow.*
— LAURA PALMER

Our youthful dreams were filled with grand expectations of our impact on the world. Some of those goals were reached; many were not.

Now, it's easier to accept that not all our plans will come to pass. In accepting that, we are able to set new goals that better reflect our dreams and ideals today. For a while it may seem as though we are "just surviving," but we can have more.

At our stage of life we are capable of making mature decisions, of setting more realistic goals. Each day we can reflect upon our accomplishments and upon the joy of family, friends, and work. Finally, we can feel comfortable with ourselves, and we can look forward to our tomorrows.

*Yesterday is gone and unchangeable,
but today is real and is mine to use.*

～ MARCH 10 ～

You cannot teach a man anything.
You can only help him find it within himself.
—GALILEO

We can't avoid the crises, large or small, that are a normal part of living. Automobile accidents, spending more money than we can afford, stubbed toes, rain on vacations—these things happen to everyone. No one is exempt. But we can learn from our negative experiences. We learn to be more careful, to hold our tongues, to be more responsible.

No one can teach us how to live. We have to learn by ourselves. And eventually we're better able to handle our own problems, sometimes even with grace and finesse. We can share what we have learned with others, we can help pave the way for them, but invariably they, too, will have to do it for themselves.

Life hands me situations. I have the ability to
make them into positive experiences.

~ MARCH 11 ~

The hopeful man sees success where others see failure,
sunshine where others see shadows and storm.
—O. S. MARDEN

Once in a while we lose sight of the world around us and get caught up in how miserable we are feeling. We may be in physical or emotional pain and become self-absorbed. Or we may be unhappy because things are not going exactly the way we want.

But we can imagine, just for a moment, a beautiful watercolor picture of a sunrise—the promise of a brand-new day. The hues are gentle pastels. The colors blend together subtly, gently, with no perceptible break from one section to another. We can relax in the beauty and serenity of the scene. We can enjoy it with no other motive than pleasure. Positive imagery can help us enhance the beauty of the moment.

I am overwhelmed by nature's beauty and by the
great joy I feel. I can call back these same feelings
by visualizing them in my mind.

Never bend your head. . . .
Look at the world straight in the face.
—HELEN KELLER

Pride is elusive when we're hurting emotionally. We may act and feel overwhelmed. It is very difficult to be mindful of all we can accomplish, and we may focus on what is out of our reach. Or we may tend to hide from our problems by withdrawing from social gatherings or by isolating ourselves emotionally. Feeling ashamed that we are hurting makes asking for help very hard.

Now, as we hide less often from our feelings, we find it easier to face the world straight on. We may not have made this transition easily or even by ourselves, but we are making it with the help of loving friends. Increasingly, we accept our limitations, make the effort to do what we can, and ask for help when we must. And with this, we raise our heads with pride.

I need not be ashamed when I must ask others for help.

~ MARCH 13 ~

The longer I live the more beautiful life becomes.
—FRANK LLOYD WRIGHT

When we were younger, day and night were two separate entities. Day was when we played, and night was when we slept. The distinction is not that sharp as we get older, especially if we have any problems which disturb our sleep. Worry and pain have a tendency to make nights much longer—and lonelier.

What looked hopeless the night before can take on a whole new light in the morning. It would be wonderful if we could learn to treat each new day with the same freshness we had as children. We can learn, once again, to experience and to savor each moment. Once we separate night and day, the way we did years ago, we are more likely to allow ourselves wonderful days again.

My expectations are that I will
achieve the best each day has to offer.

⌣ MARCH 14 ⌣

A cheerful face is nearly as good for an invalid
as healthy weather.
— BENJAMIN FRANKLIN

Health changes, like other changes in life circumstances, can undermine friendships. When we are dealing with chronic pain or discomfort or when we have become impaired with illness, some friends just aren't sure how to act under the new circumstances.

People who love us want to help us; they want to be with us. The hard part for us is how to let them. Visits won't be easy for us or them at first because our lives and relationships are changed by illness. But soon we realize that we still care for and need these special people and that we want to show our affection, during the trying times as well as during the better times.

I can find comfort and stability by
maintaining my friendships.

~ MARCH 15 ~

A man without a plan for the day is lost before he starts.
—Lewis K. Bendele

Some mornings we are tempted, especially when we are having more than our usual share of pain, to resist the demands and responsibilities of the day before us. We are enticed by the thought of making a cup of coffee, climbing back into bed with the newspaper, and hiding from the world.

Although tempting, this is usually not a good plan for us, and what we need is a plan that encourages us to live the day fully. We may actually have to contrive a plan to push us into action. Personal care, chores needing to be done, letters or phone calls to friends, a trip to the store for groceries—these emphasize our importance and the importance of the day. Without a plan, we risk wasting twenty-four hours in loneliness and self-pity.

I and this day are important, and my plan reflects this.

Time ripens all things. No man's born wise.
— CERVANTES

One moment in time, a phrase from an old song that still rings true. In a single moment we could decide the balance of how we will live our lives. Split-second decisions, not all good ones, permeate the fabric of our lives, of everyone's lives—regardless of medical problems.

Sometimes we are very sorry about a decision we made too quickly, a decision that may alter the course of our lives for a short while or even permanently. Perhaps the car we insisted on having is a lemon, or we may not like the new community into which we impulsively moved. We have to learn to live with our decisions, at least until we make a decision to change. Ponder a decision just a moment longer. Each experience can deepen our wisdom.

I will attempt to take my time when making decisions.

~ MARCH 17 ~

*Time is lost when we have not lived a full human life,
time unenriched by experience, creative endeavor,
enjoyment, and suffering.*
—DIETRICH BONHOEFFER

"I'll never make it through today!" While we all may
have had that thought from time to time, we did live
through that day to rise the next morning and greet the
new day. Time can go by very slowly when we are
thinking of no one but ourselves. Sometimes we can feel
overwhelmed by fear of an uncertain future. We may
even feel that we have been deserted by our friends and
family in a time of need.

When overwhelmed with these helpless feelings, we
can turn to our Higher Power for comfort and understanding. Knowing we don't have to work through the
details of our lives alone not only comforts us, it fills our
minutes and days with positive thoughts and actions.

*My Higher Power lends me strength
to carry me through.*

∽ MARCH 18 ∽

*An ordinary man can surround himself
with two thousand books . . .
and thenceforward have at least one place
in the world in which it is possible to be happy.*
—AUGUSTINE BIRRELL

A flashlight. A winter storm. Secretly reading under the covers. As children, most of us escaped into books from time to time. Books were a private experience, shared with no one. They could also be a warm family time of sharing.

Books still provide a window to the world, to adventures and faraway places that few people ever experience firsthand. Regardless of physical ability—or disability—we can generally find a way to read or listen to a book. We can shed, for a short while, some of the frustrations we experience. We can forget the ravages of illness. We can travel. We can dream.

Reading is a true gift which I can give myself.

*Faith in a holy cause is to a considerable extent
a substitute for the lost faith in ourselves.*
—ERIC HOFFER

Busy! Busy! Busy! We might feel as though we're living our lives on a treadmill—always on the go, helping and giving our time to people and causes.

Service and volunteerism can be wonderful ways to help, but only if they augment an already full life. We truly are living on a treadmill if our involvement is an escape from facing our innermost thoughts and fears. We are getting nowhere if our outside activities are all we have to wake up for each morning.

We begin to change when we honestly face our greatest fears. We can search our personalities to find our vulnerable points and then strive to correct what defects we can. It is then that we regain faith in ourselves and in our abilities.

*Once I regain faith in myself,
I can open my heart to help others.*

∼ MARCH 20 ∼

Understanding human needs
is half the job of meeting them.
—ADLAI STEVENSON

We may have needed constant reminding to do our chores when we were children. We expected to be told what to do. Today we are adults and are chronically ill, and we find ourselves giving reminders to the people around us. Now, however, the suggestions have to be extremely delicate and carefully given.

We can gently guide the behavior of our spouse, friends, parents, and children regarding our medical problems. Our comments can be honest and direct: "It would help me if you would let me try to do things for myself before offering me your help." Or, "Please sweep the floor." Or, "Would you put the towels into the dryer?" Those around us are not able to read our minds. We can learn to say "I need" or "I want." Our needs will be met if we ask directly.

Learning to ask for help is hard, but I can learn.

It is a happy talent to know how to play.
—Ralph Waldo Emerson

As the carefree days of childhood give way to adulthood, we sometimes forfeit too much of the child. We become what we think is mature—serious and busy. Quite unintentionally we might become caught up in the importance of being married, working hard at our jobs, raising children, or paying off the mortgage. Even at home we might be rushing here and there—mowing the lawn, getting a haircut, buying clothes or groceries, and performing all the small household chores which need doing regularly.

Where is the time we need for ourselves, to spend with friends, or just to play? We can find time, right now, if we want to. We can momentarily shrug off the demands of home or career and lend ourselves to carefree play.

It's sometimes easy to be too serious.
Today, I will let myself participate in play.

Courage is the resistance to fear,
mastery of fear, not absence of fear.
— MARK TWAIN

So many of us suffer from flagging self-esteem. This may occur for many reasons, all complex. When we finally decide we are going to create change in our lives, we may be uncertain as to how to make the change. How do we start? One of the best ways to start is to adopt one premise of the Twelve Step programs and begin to act "as if" we have all the confidence in the world, "as if" we have great faith in ourselves. We start to spend time thinking about the possibilities, rather than the impossibilities.

We all fear the unknown, but to act "as if" helps us deal with the things we can't see. Eventually, contrived as it feels, our new behavior will become a new habit, and we won't need to act "as if" because we truly "are."

I am willing to try to act "as if" I can create change.

～ MARCH 23 ～

There the weary cease from troubling,
and there the weary be at rest.
—JOB 3:17

We never thought we would have to learn to live with constant weariness. Our notions of illness may have prepared us for pain, inconvenience, maybe even some negative emotions like anger, but we had no way of anticipating the unrelenting drain of illness. There is tremendous comfort just in knowing we are not alone, that ultimately there is a Power greater than ourselves to whom we can turn for comfort and strength.

We can't always escape the physical weariness of illness, but we can regenerate our spirituality, which may have dissipated along with our good health.

I cannot control my illness,
but I can have a hopeful attitude.

⌒ MARCH 24 ⌒

Our safety is not in blindness,
but in facing our danger.
—JOHANN CRISTOPH SCHILLER

Sometimes our difficulties are compounded when we take more drugs than needed to treat our illnesses. This can be due to our getting prescriptions from more than one doctor or from using over-the-counter drugs in addition to our prescribed medications.

Certainly, we need to use the drugs that will keep us as healthy and functional as possible, but over-medication can be an accidental side-effect of chronic medical problems. Also, psychological or physical dependence can also occur.

Besides necessary medications, the joy of living and the love of ourselves and others can help us deal with our illnesses. By learning to live with our limitations we can regain some of the personal power that chronic illness has taken from us.

I am strengthened by facing my problems.

*Every man takes the limits of his own field of vision
for the limits of the world.*
—ARTHUR SCHOPENHAUER

It's not easy to get used to the idea of a "forever" kind of illness. When we first learned about it, we may have allowed it to overtake our lives. Perhaps we lost the pleasure of taking a walk, playing a card game with friends, or spending time helping others. We were obsessed with the memory of how life used to be.

We can learn to put illness into its correct position. We have the chronic condition; it doesn't own us. We will know we have reached true acceptance when the medical issue doesn't dominate our days.

Of course a chronic illness affects us, but now we can see it properly as only one facet of our lives. We can choose to once again have full and meaningful days.

*I—not my illness—can choose
how well and how fully I will live my life.*

This confrontation with death . . .
makes everything look so precious, so sacred,
so beautiful, that I feel more strongly than ever
the impulse to live it, to embrace it,
and to let myself be overwhelmed by it.
—ABRAHAM MASLOW

When we are ill, we are forced to face our own mortality. A close brush with death is enough to put the fear of dying into us, but with this fear a sense of spirituality may flow through our lives. Problems, which once seemed overwhelming, diminish in size. The trees are greener; the sky is bluer. People are kinder and more sharing than ever before.

We often don't appreciate what we've taken for granted until it's nearly yanked away from us. All of a sudden, every day is a gift. Every day is a precious chance to live.

I am continuing the struggle to make each day
the best one because I rejoice in the gift of life.

～ MARCH 27 ～

Patience is the best remedy for every trouble.
— PLAUTUS

We are used to the quick fix. Candy bars hold back our hunger. Credit cards allow us to spend freely when we are financially strapped. We drive through the fast-food lanes and eat on the way to our next stop.

And when we were told about our illness, our reaction may have been, "Okay. Now how can it be fixed?" We were told that part of the treatment was time, a remedy requiring patience and one difficult to accept. We are learning to accept that the nature of our illnesses requires us to be patient. We can use this patience to slow our often frantic behavior and to notice the value in each passing minute. Our time becomes more and more precious as we understand that patience is a very good remedy.

Today, I can begin to practice patience.

It is not death or pain that is to be dreaded,
but the fear of pain or death.
—EPICTETUS

The pain we anticipate—whether it be a flu shot, a lengthy dental procedure, or surgery—is usually worse than the actual pain. Perhaps this is because the anticipation of pain includes fear or dread.

As we deal with pain, we may find healthier ways to cope with it. Once, even the sense of a headache coming might have caused us to tense our muscles and prepare for the onslaught. Now, we're more likely to settle down to begin thinking of positive imagery or relaxation therapy. We are giving ourselves the moments we need to be alone, to breathe deeply, to think of a beautiful and calming sight. We're learning to relax and be less fearful.

I need to remind myself of my personal power.
I can exercise control over my body
and strive to minimize the effects of fear.

⚬ MARCH 29 ⚬

Happiness should not depend on physical wellness.
— K. O'Brien

Without even recognizing that we have done so, we sometimes structure our entire lives on the foundation of good health. We assume good health for our future. And we refuse to even acknowledge that nature's somewhat random selection process can change the way we live. We may never even give a moment's thought to changing our habits because of illness. We feel exempt, confident it will never happen to us.

And when it does and our lifestyle changes—sometimes gradually, sometimes abruptly—we feel we've lost the right to happiness. Then we begin to adjust. Family and friends stick with us, and an awareness comes forth that they, not physical activity, are the reasons for true happiness.

I accept and will adjust to chronic illness.
Poor health has changed my life, not ended it.

*If you don't learn to laugh at trouble, you won't have
anything to laugh at when you grow old.*
—ED HOWE

Laughing with others is important. Learning to laugh at
our own problems, however, is even more important.
Since we will continue to live with situations that cause
us all types of problems, we may as well learn to laugh
at ourselves.

Often with chronic illness, coordination changes.
Reaction time may be slower. Sensitivity to cold, heat,
or pain may be altered. It's only logical that we will find
ourselves in potentially embarrassing situations because
of our bodies.

Often, a hearty laugh at all the strange situations
flung our way is just the thing to help us work through
what is painful and difficult. Laughter is a gift we give to
ourselves. We can carry it with us wherever we go, and
it will always be ours.

I am headed in the right direction when I can laugh.

～ MARCH 31 ～

Why, why, why?
—JAMES JOYCE

"It doesn't seem fair," we privately lament. "How could I have this rotten medical condition just when I've hit my stride—the prime time of my life?"

That's a question we all wonder about. Many of us may get down on our knees and pray to our Higher Power for understanding. We might ask, "Why me?" We might implore, "Why now, when I'm nearly on my feet again?"

We might ask these questions, yet often there are no answers. Our ways are not His ways. Sometimes life just isn't fair; there are no easy answers.

I have adjusted to other changes in my life,
and I can adjust to this one too.
It may take some time, and I may go through the
gamut of emotions first, but I am willing.

～ APRIL 1 ～

Spring is a happiness so beautiful,
so unique, so unexpected,
that I don't know what to do with my heart.
—EMILY DICKINSON

Remember the sheer joy of spring during childhood? How we would race around the backyard, checking out the wonderful sights and smells? Spring in those days meant no more snow pants and boots. It meant being able to dash out with just a light sweater and no admonishments from Mom. And most important, the new season heralded a few short months until summer vacation.

We can recapture our youthful openness, for that child is still within us. We can smell the same scents, experience the same joy, but with the depth of understanding we have gained as adults. Regardless of our level of independence, regardless of whether we can plant the garden or just enjoy its flowers, spring can still delight us.

My heart still delights in spring.
I am grateful to be here to absorb it all.

⌒ APRIL 2 ⌒

*The joy of life is to put out one's power
in some natural and useful or harmless way.
There is no other, and the real misery is not to do this.*
—OLIVER WENDELL HOLMES, JR.

If our health changes and fatigue are frequent problems, we may become unable to do all we did for ourselves in the past. If we push ourselves too far, something will suffer. We may pay with sore joints or we may pay with depression. But we do pay.

If we liken our daily energy level to money in a bank account, we realize we can make only so many withdrawals before our resources run out. We decide each day how we want to spend—or waste—that precious energy. It takes a while to get our priorities rearranged, but living a good life is important, and eventually we learn how to invest our energy well.

*Each day presents itself new and fresh.
It's up to me to decide how to spend my energy.*

~ APRIL 3 ~

Excessive fear is always powerless.
—AESCHYLUS

Something may be interfering with our sleep. Eyes wide, we lie in bed night after night. We move through the days like robots, just getting by. Our lack of sleep may stem from worries and problems that we can't face.

Our confrontation with illness may have suddenly made us see how powerless we are over some parts of our lives. Where once we had felt that everything had an acceptable answer, we now have to live with an answer we don't like and we can't change. We may pull that original sense of helplessness into other areas of our lives. Gradually, we understand that life has always been unpredictable; we just refused to see it until we were forced to. We learn to accept the things we can't change and work toward changing the things we can. We deal with our problems. Our anxiety subsides. We're able to rest.

Today, I'll accept unchangeable answers.

～ APRIL 4 ～

The mind leaps,
and leaps perhaps with a sort of elation.
—JOSEPH WOOD KRUTCH

A chronic medical problem can be incorporated into our total picture of life. If we allow problems, medical or otherwise, to overwhelm and exclude everything else, we are defeated before we begin. We don't have to be defeatists.

Every day dawns fresh with opportunities to change, to find happiness, and to live our lives well. By searching deeply within, we can redefine our faith in ourselves and in our Higher Power. A joy, an elation, can be ours when we allow ourselves to express our natural human curiosity through growth, learning, and a willingness to try new things. We can hold our heads up high and be proud.

Regardless of my physical condition,
I have dignity and worth.

～ APRIL 5 ～

Be not afraid to pray, to pray is right.
Pray, if thou canst with hope, but even pray.
—HARTLEY COOLIDGE

"Now I lay me down to sleep" may have been one of our first childhood prayers, perhaps even one of our first memories. As we grew, we may have learned to recite other prayers by rote, with little understanding.

Now, we are beginning to understand and feel the need for prayer. Many of us came to believe in a Power greater than ourselves, one which can nurture and sustain us. We can pray for those we love; we can pray for ourselves. Prayer can enhance and bond us with our Higher Power. It nourishes and satisfies our souls—our inner self.

Prayer is a creative expression of my spiritual needs.
It offers me a deep sense of personal satisfaction
and continually reminds me of all life's forces.

～ APRIL 6 ～

The man who makes no mistakes
does not usually make anything.
—EDWARD JOHN PHELPS

We feel so vulnerable when we have a chronic illness, almost as though we are specimens, displayed as oddities. Because of our vulnerable feelings, we may be reluctant to undertake new experiences out of fear that we may expose ourselves to ridicule. Yet, actually, few people take the time or trouble to stare.

Living a sequestered life and taking no chances is not the answer. There are always options available to us, but they may be different options from those we previously considered. We can decide to take new directions. The image we show to others is a reflection of the image we carry within.

Trying to reach past my mistakes
into new successes enhances my life.

⌒ APRIL 7 ⌒

Sometimes I have believed as many as
six impossible things before breakfast.
—LEWIS CARROLL

While sitting at the table with an early morning cup of tea or coffee, we can get lost in reverie. Briefly, for a frozen moment in time, we can believe that we are capable of anything once again.

We still have the joy of our imagination, and even if there are physical restrictions placed upon us by our long-term medical conditions, we can still imagine ourselves achieving an impossible dream. It's wonderful to get lost in pure fantasy about how we would like our lives to be. We can imagine ourselves richer in relationships and in friends. Even when our bodies betray us, we need never betray the belief in ourselves.

I have the freedom to imagine whatever I want.
My illness doesn't restrict what I can
accomplish in my mind.

∽ APRIL 8 ∽

Believe me, every man has his secret sorrow,
which the world knows not, and oftentimes
we call a man cold when he is only sad.
—HENRY WADSWORTH LONGFELLOW

Let a person seem aloof or display a need to be apart from others, and we automatically assume we are getting a cold shoulder. Yet none of us has any idea of all the components of another person's life and feelings. We're usually ignorant of other people's personal characteristics. Sadness, shyness, and fear are just a few traits that can be misinterpreted.

Little disappointments, large failures, loss of a dream or a loved one—these are all problems that any one of us can have, but few can share. We can choose to overlook the real and imagined wrongs of others by reminding ourselves of how little we really know of each other.

My understanding of other people's problems
has been enhanced by my own illness,
and I will not be so quick to judge.

～ APRIL 9 ～

The comforter's head never aches.
—ITALIAN PROVERB

Sometimes, people who undergo a family crisis, such as the sudden death of a loved one, hold up commendably during the most difficult times, only to collapse later. While none of us can always stay calm, we rarely buckle when our strength is needed by others.

We comfort our loved ones when they're angry, hurt, or disappointed. We comfort friends who have undergone surgery or had other crises of their own. We sit by the bed of people we love as they wait to die. Again and again, we prove we are strong. Our experience in comforting others helps us recognize the strength of our friends and family when they comfort us in our anger or disappointment, in our sadness or illness.

I am proud I can give comfort and strength to those who need it. I am grateful for those who comfort me.

~ APRIL 10 ~

A friend is a person with whom I may be sincere.
Before him, I may think aloud.
— RALPH WALDO EMERSON

We may wonder what has happened to old friends we have lost touch with over the years. Sometimes we get so caught up in our busy lives we neglect our friendships.

We can rebuild or strengthen a relationship by taking the first step in reaching out to others. Old connections can be reestablished. They were important to us at one time in our lives and can be again. We may find that our old friends have been wondering about us as well.

Today, we can take up pen and paper and write to them about ourselves. Now is the time to find out what has happened to our old friends and let them know they're in our thoughts.

I will try today to establish contact with an old friend.

~ APRIL 11 ~

*When you get into a tight place, and everything
goes against you, till it seems as though you could not
hold on a moment longer, never give up then,
for that is just the place and time that the tide will turn.*
—HARRIET BEECHER STOWE

Sometimes we push ourselves too fast, too far, too often. Even though we are cognizant of that exact moment when we just cannot, physically or emotionally, go on any longer, we still persevere.

When we finally do acknowledge that once again we have gone too far, it may be time to take a nap or exercise to release our emotions. Or we may choose to be with friends or family. We begin to understand that the bad times pass.

If we can just make it through one more moment, then the tables will turn in our favor.

I am able to make it through even the hardest hard day.

⌣ APRIL 12 ⌣

A crisis event often explodes the
illusions that . . . anchor our lives.
—ROBERT VENINGA

Chronic illness can become so commonplace for us that we lull ourselves into thinking we've become the best we can be and believing we can handle everything. When another crisis occurs—family problems, financial setbacks, or loss of friends—we may stubbornly try to fix the situation, only to be rewarded with self-pity or anger or sadness.

In time, we usually realize that we don't have to carry every burden or solve every problem. Sometimes there is no answer other than acceptance of a situation as being unchangeable. What can be changed is our reaction to this fact. We can, as we have before, build our lives around the new situation. We can allow ourselves to grow into a greater maturity.

Every day, every experience is an opportunity to grow.

Tears are summer showers to the soul.
—ALFRED AUSTIN

All our lives, we have been told that time would heal all wounds—and that if time couldn't, then the doctor would.

There are few things that may feel as final as a diagnosis of chronic illness. Chronic means forever—and we can hardly conceive of a problem that will never go away. We may find ourselves crying over and over again, and wonder if the tears will ever end.

For many of us, our tears were how we began to grieve. Grief was how we started to heal ourselves emotionally from the burden of "forever." The tears we shed helped cleanse our thoughts and bodies so we could move on to live the rest of our lives. Today, our grief and weeping will help us continue to grow.

I can let myself shed the purifying tears that well up in my heart. They will help me move on with my life.

You are the handicap you must face.
You are the one who must choose your place.
—JAMES ALLEN

Each of us carries a handicap, although some handicaps are more obvious than others. They can be physical limitations, but they can also be emotions, feelings, or attitudes that impede the full enjoyment and promise of living. A handicap may be an image problem or dismay at how we walk or talk, or it could be chronic illness. And we certainly can have more than one handicap.

A full life depends on our ability to cope with our difficulties and to decide whether any of them are self-imposed. We haven't chosen all our limitations—physical or emotional—but we can choose to strip our lives of the ones we've created. And we can choose how we will respond to the others.

I will define my special place in the world,
and I will try to meet my own best expectations.

～ APRIL 15 ～

Just because everything is different,
doesn't mean anything has changed.
—IRENE PETER

Change may happen gradually without our being aware
of it. A sudden event may force us to recognize how different our lives have become. Yet even when the details
or circumstances have changed, we may discover that
the real meaning of our lives has remained the same.

We still carry many of the same values as before. We
are thankful for the stable relationships that have grown
as we have become stronger. We still strive to succeed
in the goals we've set. We continue to look for—and to
find—meaning in our life experiences. Certainly, we've
changed and many things are different, but we continue
to carry within ourselves the unique person we each
are, the person we've always been.

I have always been a person capable of
tremendous growth. I'm thankful that I can make
changes that will help me grow.

*Any real progress in the tangled world of emotions
must be made by the individual.
Each of us must hold the mirror to our own soul
and gaze intently at what we see there.*
— BERNARD S. RASKAS

"Making do" is an old-fashioned phrase that signifies our ability to manage with whatever we have. We have all thought of that phrase in terms of food, money, or clothes, but rarely in terms of health.

If we have not begun to cope with our limitations, we may find ourselves wallowing in the negativity of self-pity or anger. We may become so entangled in these self-defeating thoughts that we lose our ability to grow and to see other real choices. Instead of raging at the unfairness of poor health or limited mobility, we can "make do" with the strength, time, ability, and creativity we still have.

*I will use what I have
and not bemoan what I don't have.*

⟶ APRIL 17 ⟵

The great and glorious masterpiece of man
is to know how to live to purpose.
— Montaigne

When we undergo any crisis, it's quite common for self-esteem to take a plunge. If life seems to hand us one crisis after another, our feelings of self-worth may vary from day to day. Once we get used to the newest change (perhaps this time it is diminished health), we begin to realize that only we are capable of nurturing ourselves.

We can solve some of our problems by setting new, more realistic goals, goals that we can reach. Then our damaged self-esteem can start to become whole once again.

I am capable of taking better care of myself by
setting challenging goals and by doing things I love to do.

～ APRIL 18 ～

He who conceals his disease cannot expect to be cured.
—ETHIOPIAN PROVERB

We gain very little if we use our problems to hide from other people and the realities of life. Yet, at times, we may drift into this negative attitude even though a reclusive life is self-serving, not the least bit enjoyable, and unfair to the people who care about us.

One way to survive is to develop the confidence we need to face others. Our problems should not be the first impression people have of us, but that is all we present if we are hiding our real selves from them. We have so much to offer—and so much to gain—when we set ourselves out on center stage and actively get on with living.

I am capable of buoying myself up to face each new challenge by moving out of my hiding places.

*The only courage that matters is the kind that
gets you from one moment to the next.*
—MIGNON MCLAUGHLIN

Morning sounds and sights filter in through the bedroom window as we lie awake wondering, once again, if
we can get started for the day. "Oh," we think to ourselves, "can I make these tired and weary bones and
these sore and aching muscles do what I command them
to do one more time?"

We need strength to begin, to face each day, to start
working our joints so we can face another day. A silent
prayer may rush from our lips as we gather all our resources. We are extraordinarily strong people. Having a
health problem makes us aware of a source of strength
previously left untapped. We open ourselves to that
strength—within ourselves, our doctors, our Higher
Power. We rise and get on with our lives.

*I have two gifts right now — this day and the strength
to meet its challenges and demands.*

My mind to me a kingdom is,
Such present joys therein I find
That it excels all other bliss
That earth affords or grows by kind.
—Sir Edward Dyer

Within the private confines of our thoughts, we can build castles or dream of solving all the problems of the world. At times, we may still daydream like children who envision themselves as heroes, builders, or saviors. We may still unconsciously look for drama and excitement.

Maturity gives us something that our youthful selves would never have understood—compromise. We don't have to see compromise as surrender. For us, it can mean action. When faced with the reality of dreams that can't be achieved, we can compromise by building new dreams that not only are as important as our original ones, but also offer success.

My dreams can still direct the course of my life.

To know
That which lies before us in daily life,
Is the prime wisdom.
—John Milton

It isn't easy becoming an adult. We have to pay the dues as we go along the path of life. As long as we have had joy and suffering, we may as well learn to use our well-earned adult perspective. After all, look how hard we worked to get here!

Enjoyment is still there, free for the taking. All the intangibles we enjoyed before are still there—love, honor, trust. We alone can decide, as we sift through the happenings of our days, whether to call our lives wreckage or success, whether to create delight or sorrow. A change in circumstances or health doesn't mean the end of joyful living. Such changes will often help us to begin living our lives more wisely, with greater appreciation and understanding.

I will find and accept the gift of joyful living today.

*As mature people we must learn not to love ourselves
excessively nor to mistrust the universe morbidly.*
—Joshua Loth Liebman

Each time we know success, large or small, we may tend
to applaud ourselves. We have all seen small children
clapping their hands together in glee at some small
triumph. That is the spontaneity of human nature.

Even now that we are older, we may find it difficult
not to praise ourselves in front of others each time we
make some kind of gain. We learn we are applauded for
those special times with which all people can identify—
success on the job or when a new child or grandchild
is born. Sometimes, however, our applause must be
private—treasured by no one but ourselves—for we may
be the only ones to realize how much we deserve it.

*When I achieve success, in any aspect of my life,
I will glow with inner pride.*

～ APRIL 23 ～

To everything there is a season,
and a time to every purpose under the heaven.
—ECCLESIASTES 3:1

All times and places in our lives have meaning and value. Regardless of what we have done in the past, whether we are proud or ashamed of our past actions, the only time over which we have any control is now. If we have no sense of direction in life, if we have no daily power or purpose, we may wander aimlessly through this new time in our lives, unaware of where we are going.

The reality of our lives is this: Our health has changed. We are the only ones who can choose how to deal with this reality. We can wistfully look back to another time and place, or we can live in the here and now by making the best of a less-than-ideal situation. The choice is ours, but only the second choice provides our lives with meaning and purpose.

I won't squander today by living in the past.

～ APRIL 24 ～

To struggle when hope is banished.
To live when life's salt is gone!
To dwell in a dream that's vanished—
To endure, and go calmly on!
—BEN JONSON

At times we all dwell in the mansions created by our own dreams. When dream rooms are the only ones we visit, however, reality will jar us back to the present. We then have only two choices: to move forward or to live continually in the past.

Just when it seems there is no future, that there is no chance to ever live a normal life again, a thread of hope surfaces, and we struggle onward. Recognition that we can—and are—still enduring gives rise to hope and helps us go calmly on.

Dreams are sacred to me, but I must live
in the present so I can survive day to day.

~ APRIL 25 ~

Every tub must stand on its own bottom.
— THOMAS FULLER

As we accomplish each goal in our lives, we feel a tremendous sense of pride. Whether from success at the job, in school, or in a volunteer capacity, achieving a goal is personally gratifying.

The challenge that chronic illness presents is to reorganize our goals so they are still practical and attainable. If we spend our time complaining rather than changing, we may never learn to live successfully with the illness. It's not going to go away. Things will never be the same as before. Accepting this fact is a colossal challenge.

My faith in myself has waned with the onset of my illness. I am just realizing that I can still depend on myself.

Kindness can become its own motive.
We are made kind by being kind.
—ERIC HOFFER

Our own simple words to others can brighten our day. Too often we are caught up in the personal miseries of our lives, too involved to reach out to other people. We may forget that other people have the same needs we do. So many times, because we are ill or old or hurting, we expect others to come to us. That's not fair to them, and it's not good for us.

Kind words and actions toward others can help us through the hard times. We can smile at the elderly man all alone in the grocery checkout line. We can talk to neighbors, thank the young man who courteously holds a door open, and reach out in dozens of other ways to the people who even briefly touch our lives. It's good for them—and for us.

I will make an extra effort to reach out
in kindness to my neighbors and friends.

～ APRIL 27 ～

Solitude:
A good place to visit, but a poor place to stay.
—JOAN BILLINGS

We probably recognize our need for solitude in our lives—private time when we can sit and think, or listen to music, or simply enjoy the quiet. When solitude becomes a way of life, however, it can lead to loneliness, and loneliness can lead to self-pity. This is a dangerous position.

We tread a real tightrope with our need for solitude. We need to be alone, but not isolated. In our solitude, we can find serenity through meditation and prayer. Once we are reenergized, it will be easier for us to balance our lives by inviting a friend into our home or reaching out to another who is in pain. Solitude encourages us to turn our backs on loneliness and to reach out to others once again.

I will not impose a sentence of solitary confinement
upon myself. I am still a valuable member of society.

Where there's music, there can be no evil.
—CERVANTES

So many of us spent part of our childhoods glued to the radio, ears alert for our favorite stories and songs. Listening to music filled large parts of our days. The joy of music need not ever dim.

We can let the song within our hearts burst forth, unbidden, to warm the memories of our souls and the texture of our days. Bubbling to the surface of awareness, music can create a twinkle in the eyes and cause a smile to burst into full bloom even on the shiest person's face.

We can use the magic of music to uplift a bad mood or dissipate our sadness. While listening to music, we can, for a while, forget our problems. Loving music is a special source of happiness we can carry with us wherever we go.

My warmest feelings can surface as I listen to or play music, and I can feel perfectly happy.

*You grow up the day you have
the first real laugh — at yourself.*
—ETHEL BARRYMORE

If we are always serious and never see the funny side of life, there will be no respite from our illnesses. It takes fewer muscles to laugh than to cry. We'll breathe easier and deeper, and we'll be much more content when we laugh.

We can choose to pay attention to why other people are laughing and learn to laugh along with them. We can try every day—even every hour—to find the positive or humorous side of life, for laughter helps us put things into perspective. It lends hope and meaning to life.

*I will open my eyes to the funny side of life
and laugh with others.*

~ APRIL 30 ~

Although the world is full of suffering,
it is also full of the overcoming of it.
—HELEN KELLER

It's easy to become overwhelmed with the day-to-day pain and annoyance of a chronic medical condition. We try hard, but every now and again our perspective gets knocked off center. We may begin to think only in terms of sickness and pain.

Sometimes it's difficult to find a kind thought or a warm spot for ourselves. If we shadow our lives with pain, frustration, and scorn, we will not be able to relax within the quiet confines of our days. Each day is new and fresh, and it's up to us to welcome it with joy and gratitude. It's up to us to overcome the obstacles to our happiness.

Today, I take the responsibility for my own happiness.

⌁ MAY 1 ⌁

*Blossoms are scattered by the wind
and the wind cares nothing,
but the blossoms of the heart no wind can touch.*
—Yoshida Kenko

Our personal, private, or spiritual emotions are like unfolded blossoms within us. There, too, are other, less private emotions. The love and caring we harbor for those people who are closest to us are full-blooming flowers that give us everlasting joy.

While we may not react with any emotion to blossoms blowing in the wind, we may find ourselves ever awed as those very blossoms start as buds and then bloom within a summer season. The wonders of nature are like miracles—so are the wonders of humankind.

*My innermost emotions blossom and grow within me
and bear the fruit of maturity and love for others.*

～ MAY 2 ～

*Wisdom denotes the pursuing of
the best ends by the best means.*
—FRANCIS HUTCHESON

Remember when we were youngsters and used to say, "When I grow up, I'm going to . . ."? Somehow that magic moment never arrives. We grow a little each day, but change comes slowly.

We realize we have matured when we recognize our days as a series of options. Diminished health may change those options somewhat, but we still have choices to make.

We do not have a choice over the state of our health, but we can "grow into" acceptance and more positive attitudes. We can achieve the best for ourselves.

*Although some of my choices will be
different from those I had originally planned,
I can choose the best that life has to offer me now.*

⌒ MAY 3 ⌒

In our own secret hearts we each and all of us
feel superior to the rest of the world, or,
if not superior, at least "different" with a difference
that is very precious and beautiful to us,
and the base of all our pride and perseverance.
—SOLOMON EAGLE

How alike we all are, yet how different. Differences are what make each person so special. All our efforts and all our experiences can shine forth ready to enhance our lives and the lives of others when we dare to let our differences show.

In this complex world, each of us and our differences are needed. To find where our uniqueness is most useful, we may have to go out of our way. We may need to actually create a niche for ourselves as we have done so many times before. In doing this, we affirm our value and that of all others.

I accept my differentness as a gift
and a strength, not a weakness.

~ MAY 4 ~

. . . I was the breadwinner.
Only I didn't WIN the bread,
I worked hard, and earned it. . . .
—ELISE MACLAY

When poor health slightly alters the way we live our lives, the adjustment is difficult but feasible. But when poor health alters the way we live our lives and wrenches away even our financial livelihood, the adjustment is far more difficult.

Sufferers of chronic medical conditions often must discontinue working and may have to depend upon loved ones or disability payments for income. It may take some time to regain perspective, to realize that whether we are working or not, we still have personal worth. What matters most is what kind of person we are, not what job we do.

Life has handed me a portion I did not choose
and do not welcome, but I can choose my own response.

~ MAY 5 ~

Learn to like what you are,
for you take yourself with you wherever you go.
—K. O'BRIEN

A change in physical or mental health can lower our self-esteem. One of the hardest tasks we have to face is learning to accept who we are right now, not what we wanted to be.

Every day we have the right to assure ourselves that we are doing the very best job that we can do. Acceptance of ourselves allows us a serenity we've not known before. This doesn't mean giving up; in fact, it provides a base from which we can grow. Accepting where we are and who we are today gives us the honesty to admit our deficits. It gives us the confidence to really move forward. We can be proud that we are succeeding, even with this new and unwanted burden.

My illness has not changed who I am.
The course of my life has been changed,
but my direction remains the same—forward.

∼ MAY 6 ∼

Troubles, like babies, grow larger by nursing.
—LADY HOLLAND

The more we allow ourselves to fret about our troubles, the larger they appear to grow. Soon they are blown out of proportion.

Perhaps we need to set some time aside each day specifically for worrying. It's much easier to put our worrisome thoughts out of our minds if we know that we will deal with them at a certain time every day. This "worry time" will also give us the chance to decide whether we have any control over these problems or whether we should just let them go. None of us is without problems, and if we address them with some serious thinking time each day, we should be able to free our minds for some of the more important things in our lives—like personal growth and development of values.

I will strike a happy balance between worries and joys.

*Faith has a powerful effect in helping people recover
a sense of balance, tranquility, and hope.*
—ROBERT VENINGA

It's the funniest thing about human nature: When we are well, we accept our Higher Power with few second thoughts. When we have undergone some kind of crisis, however, large numbers of people seem to lose their faith for a while. After all, who among us hasn't asked, "Why me?" when our health first took a turn for the worse? Questioning our faith is common at such a time.

A health crisis often encourages soul-searching and spiritual exploration. Life as we knew it has gone topsy-turvy, and we need time to adjust. After a while many of us return with renewed strength to our spiritual beliefs.

*My belief in my Higher Power may have
diminished for a while, but I take comfort
in knowing that belief is always there.*

～ MAY 8 ～

Leisure is the most challenging responsibility
a man can be offered.
— WILLIAM RUSSELL

We are a work-oriented society. As children, we were taught to do our homework and the chores. We may have "played house" or pretended we were "going to work."

Play, therefore, can be a real challenge, especially for adults. Keyed up from a day in the workforce or a day coping with the rigors of illness or pain, we can hardly settle down when busy thoughts crowd our consciousness. Leisure time can be a burden to us if we don't know how to creatively fill it.

Regardless of what our job is, at home or away, we can learn to set it aside when work is over. Playtime should become sacred, for it's a special time when we feed our need to be carefree and spontaneous.

Using my leisure time for play will keep me healthier,
mentally and physically.

~ MAY 9 ~

The dark, uneasy world of family life—
where the greatest can fail and the humblest succeed.
—RANDALL JARRELL

We carry so much emotional baggage from childhood into our adult lives. The sum total of all our experiences forms our personalities and, in the very essence of our being, our spiritual selves. Less often do the wonderful memories, the happier times, spring forward in our minds. The bad feelings, the sad memories, the hard times—these are what we may remember the most.

Who we came from, what we came from, shouldn't define all that we can be as adults. There may come a time when regardless of our past experiences, we can acknowledge them, put them aside, and move on with our lives.

I can put aside my past by facing my future with hope and promise. I am looking for progress, not perfection.

Life would be infinitely happier
if we could only be born at the age of eighty
and gradually approach eighteen.
—MARK TWAIN

It isn't until we add many years to our lives that we realize just how good most of us had it at eighteen. We were, by and large, only responsible for ourselves. Hindsight is always twenty-twenty.

How nice for us that the hindsight we have developed over the years can be used to our benefit now. We understand that it's natural for older people to lead and to teach the younger ones. Paying for life's experiences—joys and sorrows—hasn't all been easy. We have earned the wisdom we have now.

Since I could not be wise when I was young,
the wisdom I have gained with maturity
will serve me well as I get older.

The emotions may be endless. The more we express them, the more we may have to express.
—E. M. FORSTER

Like layers of paint, our resistance to expressing our emotions can be peeled away. Poor health may make us feel as though we don't want to expend the effort anymore. We may have withdrawn within ourselves, isolated our feelings from risk or hurt or disappointment.

Right now might be a good time to take a long, hard look at ourselves. Are we protecting ourselves by not discussing our feelings or sharing our emotions with others? Not until those outer layers of fear, loneliness, and pain are stripped away can we get in touch with our emotions. Surprising as it seems, when we let go of our feelings and start to be totally honest with ourselves, we find greater and deeper and lovelier emotions to express.

I can openly express my feelings to those closest to me.

Every day cannot be a feast of lanterns.
—CHINESE PROVERB

Many of us sometimes feel as though our lives are boring, as though each day is too predictable and routine. "I'm missing something," we may think to ourselves, or, "There has to be more to life than this."

It's those times that we can remind ourselves to think of life as a journey. As with any lengthy trip, this one, too, has days in which the scenery is monotonous and uninspiring. But we're moving; we're making progress in our personal growth; and our attitudes are improving. Routine is not a bad thing, and it can be a good element of our lives when it gives form and balance to our days. Routine is often what gives us the time and energy to tackle new projects or to make changes.

Today, I will enjoy the calmness of my life.
Within this calmness, I will dream and make plans
for making my life even fuller.

~ MAY 13 ~

Patience and fortitude conquer all things.
— RALPH WALDO EMERSON

Remember how, as children, we waited for special occasions like birthdays and holidays? The waiting seemed endless. Adults would admonish us, "Have patience. Everything comes to those who wait."

We were always more than surprised when time seemed to pass more quickly by staying busy, just as our parents had said it would. As adults, we hear that in many instances the only way to conquer a problem is to wait it out. We can do nothing else, for no matter how important the awaited event or the news is, we can no more shorten the time than we could wish a speedy arrival of our birthdays when we were young. Now, as then, our only options are to have patience and to stay busy.

Now that I am not as well as before
I am learning the true value of patience.

A true friend is the most precious of all possessions
and the one we take the least thought about acquiring.
—La Rouchefoucauld

Even with honorable intentions we may, once in a while, treat those who care about us with less respect than they deserve. When a chronic illness has entered our lives we can become obsessed with ourselves. It is difficult to be anything but self-centered at first because we are frightened and uncertain about the future.

It is then that we may alienate our closest friends with a boring daily litany of symptoms. Gradually we learn that illness is only one part of our lives and that dwelling on it serves no purpose and may damage our friendships. When our obsession with illness subsides, we become able once again to express concern and interest in others—the foundation of friendship.

My friendships are invaluable.
I will let my friends know how much I cherish them.

Nothing has a stronger influence psychologically on their environment, and especially on their children, than the unlived lives of the parents.
—CARL JUNG

Sometimes chronic illness emphasizes flaws in our relationships. For whatever reason—greater honesty, less tolerance, or an increased need for openness—we struggle more often with conflicting feelings toward our loved ones, especially our parents.

It can be healing for us to review our childhood years without blaming or embellishment. We can look back and realize that our parents, too, were influenced by their childhood years. Did they receive the nurturing they needed? The love they deserved? Thinking about our parents in this way reminds us to live with forgiveness for ourselves and for everyone whose lives we touch.

I will allow myself to look back on my parents with forgiveness.

⌒ MAY 16 ⌒

Life is a series of experiences, each one of which makes
us bigger, even though it is hard to realize this.
— HENRY FORD

During these most devastating periods of our lives, it is
hard to recognize that we will, in the long run, benefit
from the experience. As we live through painful or trying times when we are barely surviving, we certainly are
not aware of growing or of learning something.

Yet, in the more quiet times of our lives, when we're
not in pain or just hanging on by a thread, we can see
that, yes, I did learn this or, indeed, that event did force
me to grow. Chronic illness is no different from other
crises, and we are able to inventory ourselves and see
healthier attitudes and stronger character as results of
what we've experienced.

I will take time today to list the ways
in which some "bad" experiences have helped
me become a better or more mature person.

When you dig another out of trouble,
you find a place to bury your own.
—ANONYMOUS

When acting the way people expect us to, we may help others, but does it really come from the heart? Frequently people act not out of compassion or caring, but because that's how they feel others will expect them to behave.

When helping others in a completely unselfish manner, we need no kudos from anyone, for we have no ulterior motive other than helpfulness. Willingness to assist other people with their problems creates some freedom from our own.

I will know I have become less selfish
when I don't have a moment's hesitation
before helping another human being.

Pain is part of being alive, and we need to learn that.
Pain does not last forever, nor is it necessarily unbearable,
and we need to be taught that.
—HAROLD KUSHNER

Losing anything—a loved one, a favorite book, even a set of goals we thought were reachable—can hurt deeply. But the loss of good health is one of the greatest pains we can suffer, for it signifies the ending of what is familiar and what is expected. The pain of a long-term medical condition isn't just physical, it's also emotional. We are afraid that we will not be able to live through the change.

With time, however, we adjust to this latest loss, just as we have adjusted to others. We create new routines that allow for diminished health. As laughter filters through our days once again, we understand that even despair is not permanent.

I reach outward, extending my arms for hope.
I turn inward with the thought of helping myself.
I am getting stronger.

The thought of suicide is a great consolation:
by means of it one gets successfully through
many a bad night.
—FRIEDRICH WILHELM NIETZSCHE

Many of us pretend that the thought of suicide has never crossed our minds, but our thoughts may occasionally become morbid—and we may be frightened.

These thoughts may seem harmful, but they may actually be helpful. Thoughts of suicide can force us to recognize how much we value living.

As we contemplate the moment at which our lives would end, we struggle and notice our desire for life, although we may not understand why we have this desire. What's important is that we gave ourselves the choice of death and did not choose it. As we feel the joy of that decision, we can think more of ourselves and of our worth. We really do want to live and are strong enough to know that suicide is not an acceptable solution to our problems.

I feel joy from knowing I can choose life.

Stripped of all their masquerades,
the fears of men are quite identical:
the fear of loneliness, rejection, inferiority,
unmanageable anger, illness and death.
—Joshua Loth Liebman

Sometimes we may try to hold ourselves apart from others, pretending our uniqueness makes us superior. Underneath all our bluff and bravado we recognize that our fears are shared by all people.

We fashion our lives to protect ourselves from hurt, from displeasing those we love, and from disappointing ourselves. Our best chance for success, despite some difficult burdens, is to develop a positive attitude, an open nature, and a willingness to risk. Doing this doesn't necessarily protect us from all our fears, but it does create an honest bond with other people who also accept their human nature.

My fears don't have to isolate me;
in fact, they can be the means by which
I reach out to others.

∼ MAY 21 ∼

*Out of a sense of duty and a desire to protect a loved one,
a vicious cycle of misinterpretation, guesswork,
silence, and isolation is initiated.*
—NEIL A. FIORE

For a while we may have tried to protect our loved ones by not talking about our illnesses. We may have even secretly hoped that it would go away if we didn't talk about it. We learned, however, that this would never be and that problems often escalate if they are not dealt with.

We see more clearly now that we can't protect our family members or our friends. Trying to protect them meant denying our own feelings and ignoring theirs. We've discovered that our loved ones don't need to be— and often don't want to be—protected. And when we don't protect them, we've found that we and the people we love are growing and becoming stronger.

*I can be honest with my loved ones
about my feelings and needs.*

~ MAY 22 ~

Happiness is like time and space—
we make and measure it ourselves;
it is as fancy, as big, as little, as you please;
just a thing of contrasts and comparisons.
—GEORGE DU MARIER

Happiness is a reference point, a relative state of mind to which we compare other emotions. Being happy is one of our ultimate goals. How we get there or if we get there often depends on how we live and how we treat other people.

When we were children, many of our needs were taken care of by others. Now, it is more often we who must create our own happiness. We are no longer children dependent on others for our dreams and joys. We are adults, free to make our happiness in any form or shape we wish.

My happiness depends on me, not on others.

Prayer, crystallized in words,
assigns a permanent wave-length on which
the dialogue has to be continued.
—DAG HAMMARSKJÖLD

Many of us have all but forgotten how to pray. We don't mean to avoid prayer—it just happens. Instead of prayer, we look to ourselves for answers or to others for our well-being. Our spiritual lives have become stagnant.

The reality of illness has, for many of us, underscored the limited power we have over some areas of our lives. We have no power over diagnoses, prognoses, remissions, or side-effects of medications. Whether out of anger, pain, depression, or hopelessness, a need arises to find balance in a world suddenly gone crazy. We may then turn to a Power greater than ourselves to provide the comfort we so desperately need. We pray; we meditate. We find peace.

I don't have to carry my burdens alone.

Whatever you may be sure of, be sure of this—
that you are dreadfully like other people.
—James Russell Lowell

Scientists have long known that all human bodies have essentially the same structure. In this day and age, one person's heart—or even other organs—can be implanted into another human being's body.

Other similarities come to mind as we live the day-by-day struggles of having a long-term medical condition. We share the frustrations, the unshed tears, pain, and hopelessness with all people whose state of health is forever altered. But we also share in joy, in pleasure, in the small and large successes we all can achieve as we move on with our lives. We are different, but we are also so very much the same.

Despite my physical limitations, I am more like
all other people than I am different from them.
Today, I will look for those similarities.

Much of your pain is self-chosen. It is the bitter potion
by which the physician within you heals your sick self.
— KAHLIL GIBRAN

We rarely, if ever, think of grief in terms of loss of good health, yet each of us moves through the grieving process. We have a tendency to drive away those who are closest to us—those who are willing to share our pain—because we are unsure of how to handle our crisis.

During the period of time in which we grieve we are emotionally raw, open, and vulnerable. We may refuse help because of stubborn pride, totally unaware that the people who care about us are in pain and need to share as well. Fortunately grief passes, and while we will never be the same, we do heal.

Loss of good health is new to me, and I must learn
how to be gracious to those who care about me.

Know the true value of time;
snatch, seize, and enjoy every moment of it.
No idleness, no laziness, no procrastination,
never put off till tomorrow what you can do today.
— LORD CHESTERFIELD

Whether the memories were good or bad, we can never call back those moments which are already gone. Each special time should be savored as unique, never to be repeated again.

We may be uncertain of what our future holds, especially since we are not as well as before. By understanding the preciousness of each day, we can enhance the way we live our lives.

Each day is valuable and offers us onetime opportunities to seize that moment—to make the very most of each chance to live.

Every moment is precious.
I will make the most of each day.

*True miracles are created by men where they use the
courage and intelligence that God gave them.*
—JEAN ANOUILH

Recently a woman in Minnesota received her Ph.D. She was eighty years old. She said she needed to conquer new worlds.

The quest for learning should never end, yet all too often we feel our education ends when we are done with school. If we want something intensely enough, whether we set our sights for an education or some other goal, it's very likely we will find a way of fulfilling our needs. Sometimes in the process of getting there, we discover other tracks to follow, which may take us to a slightly different endpoint than the one we had originally envisioned. We learn, as mature adults, to accept substitutes. And still we reach as far as we are able.

*I can learn to set new goals—
ones that challenge me but don't defeat me.*

Very few live by choice.
Every man is placed in his present condition
by causes which acted without his foresight,
and with which he did not always willingly operate.
— SAMUEL JOHNSON

How does a person cope with a chronic illness? Our lives are formed by the events around us; these events often move forward of their own volition, without our permission or even our willingness. Now that the problem is obvious, living with that change will test our character.

Those of us who have learned to cope with radically altered lifestyles and who can still love, laugh, and cry are survivors. We may not like our portion in life, but we are determined to handle it well.

I haven't chosen all the changes in my life,
but I can choose to accept the changes
and to live a warm and sharing life.

~ **MAY 29** ~

*There is a period of life when we swallow a knowledge
of ourselves and it becomes either good or sour inside.*
—PEARL BAILEY

We have a tendency to hold on to those dreams, goals, and images we had when we were young. When we accept the reality of what our lives have become—good or bad—we are finally adults.

It's far easier to accept external realities than our deeper, more personal internal realities. Accepting that we are never going to be tall or agile or rich is simpler than admitting that we are selfish or angry or unkind. Perhaps the external things are easier because there is nothing we can do to change them, and we resist admitting to character defects because those can be changed. We may not like what we see, but if we swallow that bitter pill we are able to change.

*I will ignore my fear and admit to the good and bad
within me. This gives me the freedom to change.*

*I expect to pass through life but once. If, therefore,
there can be any kindness I can show, or any good thing
I can do to any fellow human being, let me do it now.*
—WILLIAM PENN

Each night, as we place our heads upon our pillows, we can think back over the day and remember the things we said or did that added pleasure to others' lives. Usually, those same words and actions add joy to our lives too.

During our lives we have passed by multiple opportunities to be kind to others—there are no second chances. But what we can do is be aware of those special opportunities now and make the very best of them.

*My new awareness of life's fleeting opportunities
will help me show my kinder side more often.*

Laughter is a tranquilizer with no side effects.
—ARNOLD GLASOW

Good friends laughing together can warm the heart of even a casual onlooker. Unlike medicine, laughter costs us nothing and can be partaken of as often as we see fit.

When illness clouds our lives, it's nice to know that one thing stays the same—we can still laugh. At ourselves. With friends. At a funny television program.

A good hearty laugh is therapy for our minds and bodies. Mirthful laughter can cause a remarkable feeling of well-being and joy. Laughter loosens all the cares and woes of the day and makes them somehow easier to bear.

*Laughing openly and spontaneously
will always make me feel better.*

~ JUNE 1 ~

Sorrows are like thunderclouds— in the distance they
look black; over our heads scarcely gray.
—Jean Paul Richter

We sometimes become consumed by worry over things
we think we need to do or decide or complete. Often,
this concern is caused by us—not our problems—
because we're trying to solve all problems and make all
decisions at once.

Seen as whole, all the events in a lifetime can be
overwhelming. Our fears, our sorrows, our anguish
over the loss of good health, the loss of time, or even the
loss of someone we loved very much, can be completely
consuming. Yet if we learn to take our sorrows one by
one, to dissect them into little pieces, we find that we
can accept our sorrows as only a part of our lives. We
still can endure. Taken one at a time, our sorrows will
dissipate into wispy, insubstantial clouds.

All things are manageable when I see them
as a series of small items.

~ JUNE 2 ~

All our reasoning ends in surrender to feeling.
—BLAISE PASCAL

In all our endeavors it is apparent that success is possible only with persistent effort. We must all pay the price to achieve any worthwhile goal. We shouldn't be surprised when negative thoughts enter our minds. These thoughts do not go away easily. We have human frailties, so our thoughts are often disorganized and feelings are too subdued or excessive. Perfection is not possible no matter how hard we try. But we can search for answers.

We can't have things both ways, so we have to make choices. We can think through the trade-off before we make a choice. Whatever our choice, we should make it and accept it. Squandered chances to solve problems may be lost forever.

I struggle with the same problems over and over again. Today, I resolve to start my search to find some answers.

⌒ JUNE 3 ⌒

There are no gains without pain.
—ADLAI STEVENSON

Parents often are surprised that their children seem to change before their very eyes. The same is true in how we deal with each day. It was frightening when we experienced the toppling of many parts of our lives which had given us comfort and which we had expected to continue to comfort us. We may have initially thought that we'd never be able to reconstruct a productive life.

But we have been able to rebuild our lives. Like toddlers, we have taken a few small steps forward each day. Day after day, we've strengthened ourselves by making steady, but small, advances. Step by step we've re-created our lives, often without recognizing our growth. Then, suddenly, we look at our lives, and we are amazed at how far we've come. Amazed—and proud.

Today, I will take time to measure my growth,
both emotionally and spiritually.

∽ JUNE 4 ∽

The supreme happiness of life
is the conviction that we are loved.
— SHAKESPEARE

Unqualified love is the assurance that, regardless of how we look or act or live, we will be loved. We don't have to earn it; we don't have to measure up to it. Many of us were lucky enough to have been loved in this way by our parents and other family members. We were hugged, we were accepted—no matter what.

Some of us weren't that lucky; we may spend a large part of our adult lives looking for that love. Fortunately, we've learned that we don't have to find it; we only have to give it—we can love ourselves in a totally unqualified manner. We can't change the events of the past, but we can change the influence of those events on the present.

The feeling of loving myself and being loved by others
warms and nurtures my life.

⤳ JUNE 5 ⤳

I make myself laugh at everything,
for fear of having to weep.
— BEAUMARCHAIS

Sometimes we may want to cry. We might even feel within our eyes the burning of tears about to come, but we don't allow them to come. Perhaps we blink them back or avert our eyes so that others won't see. After all, we may reason, someone might see and want to give us undue attention or—worse yet—pity.

As we deal with our emotions, there are two issues involved—acknowledging our emotions and showing them. We may choose not to show all our emotions to others, but we do want to recognize them ourselves. Denying our negative emotions is counterproductive to the honesty we need as we build a full life. We can give ourselves permission to feel sad as well as joyous, to be angry as well as happy. They are honest feelings.

I am at the beginning of a journey
to discover my emotions.

⌇ JUNE 6 ⌇

Prayer is not asking. It is a longing of the soul.
— MOHANDAS GANDHI

Some people have suggested that we shouldn't ask for something in prayer. Yet our need to pray is often fueled by emotional or physical pain or by confusion or doubt. Certainly we can't—certainly we shouldn't—wait for distressing situations to pass before we pray or meditate.

Our souls long for balance and serenity, and we find this when we turn our pain, doubts, and fears over to the comforting presence of our Higher Power. Often what we seek is not an answer to a question as much as a sense of being loved and understood. When we can't find these in our physical world, we reach out with our spiritual selves to a balancing presence that understands our deepest pains and fears and our greatest joys.

No matter what I express in prayer,
I am comforted in knowing I'm understood.

⌒ JUNE 7 ⌒

To know how to grow old is the masterwork of wisdom,
and one of the most difficult chapters
in the great art of living.
—HENRI FREDERIC AMIEL

We often strive to imitate people we admire—special teachers, our parents, or friends. Many older people we choose to emulate have remained productive members of their communities and have found significant ways to help people. If we can be active, busy, and helpful, we will not only enhance our lives, we will become the role models for those younger than we are.

There are some people who seem to age so gracefully that they have the ability to make everyone around them feel special. We all appreciate friends like that, and we can become that way too.

I will live my life so well
that I will become a role model for young people.

~ JUNE 8 ~

Sometimes what we think is so impossible
turns out to be possible after all.
—K. O'BRIEN

The pure joy of imagination is that it holds no bounds. Even if we are tethered by poor health, we can still believe there are better days ahead. And in truth, we can find worthwhile ways to spend our precious time and energy if we wish.

Time spent lost in thought is not wasted, for these precious moments let us remember wonderful times gone by and allow us to rehearse our role in the future. We should imagine ourselves as proud and fully capable. This may, of course, not be true, but the more we try, the better we will be able to present ourselves in public. The easier it is for us to be in public, the more often we will go out.

I am not wasting time when I daydream,
for my dreams help me accept the changes in my life
and allow me to practice for the future.

⌐ JUNE 9 ⌐

No man is an island, entire of itself.
—JOHN DONNE

It's sometimes easy to develop a sense of aloneness. During our emotional and physical lows, we might sadly or bitterly isolate from other people because we feel so different from them. Our lives seem so much more complicated than theirs.

Usually, though, we do not choose to be completely independent of others. As we go through the motions of our day, our lives are touched by many people. They are part of the normal rhythm and flow of our experience.

And we are part of theirs. In hundreds of ways, we all support and nurture each other. We share their joys and pains because we care, because we're human.

When I am in need, caring people surround me.
I will make sure that I am available for others
when they need me too.

~ JUNE 10 ~

Pain is hard to bear. . . .
But with patience, day by day,
Even this shall pass away.
—THEODORE TILTON

When emotional or physical pain becomes unbearable, the duration of each day seems longer than twenty-four hours. Any movement is intolerable; any attempt to begin the day is met with the shrilling objections of the voice of pain.

It is at this exact moment, each time it occurs, that we are tempted to give up the fight and become invalids. Then something prods us to try just one more time—just one more day. And so we struggle, and we are amazed to discover that we have successfully met and conquered another sunrise and another sunset. The strength to go on was there all the time, deep within us.

When my pain becomes greater
than I can ever remember,
I must draw on my inner resources to keep going.

～ JUNE 11 ～

What we call the beginning is often the end.
And to make an end is to make a beginning.
The end is where we start from.
— GEORGE ELIOT

Sometimes a painful ending can be the beginning of a new way of life which is a happy reality. The end of grief brings us new acceptance and balance. The end of a bad relationship might be a welcome beginning.

An ending? Or a beginning? Often the answer depends on how we choose to see it. Grown children leaving home can be a sad end, or it can be an exciting opportunity to begin living more for ourselves. A move can mean leaving old friends or meeting new ones. Almost every event in life—marriage, a new job, graduation, even a vacation—means an ending of some sort. As we face each ending, we can choose to see a new beginning.

Today, I will remember that life is made
of many new beginnings.

*Develop an expanding sense of wonder at the world,
at yourself, at God. The world will never starve for
wonders— only for the want of wonder.*
—BERNARD S. RASKAS

A crisis in our lives can make us cruel and bitter but
can also cause us to do some soul-searching. Those of
us who take inventory, who soul-search, may have a
personal awakening to our capacity for joy and giving.
Being aware of the beauty and symmetry that constantly surround us allows the horizons of our minds
to expand.

As our sense of spirituality becomes whole again, we
are aware of our impact upon others and upon nature.

*A spiritual sense of self is important in my quest to find
out who I am and what kind of person I want to be.*

～ JUNE 13 ～

A desperate disease requires a dangerous remedy.
— GUY FAWKES

Safety is important to all of us, but sometimes it is so important that we refuse to take risks. We may stay in unhealthy relationships or ignore our own or others' bizarre behavior because we're afraid of leaving the safety of our routine.

We become more willing, however, to take risks when things become desperate. Then we might take desperate measures. We might seek counseling or file for divorce in order to rescue or end a hurting relationship. If we feel emotionally upset, we might ask for professional help. That, too, involves taking a risk. These decisions don't come lightly. There is much soul-searching involved, but we're able to make the decision when we realize that safety is sometimes more dangerous than risk.

I can make choices that are good for me,
even if they threaten my safe routine.

Do not sit long with a sad friend,
When you go to a garden,
do you look at the flowers?
Spend more time with roses and jasmines.
—JELALUDDIN RUMI

Sometimes we slip over the boundary line of a close friendship. Up to that point, it may have been a real union, a true meeting of the minds. But then we might not only share our thoughts and our problems, but take on each other's problems as if they were our own. We may become obsessed with finding answers for our friends.

Just as we don't focus on the weeds in our garden, we can't see only the negative aspects of our friends' lives. We can be supportive, but we serve our friends best when we let them confront their own problems.

I will remember that friends can comfort each other,
but cannot carry the other's burdens.

～ JUNE 15 ～

*Not the power to remember, but the power to forget
is a necessary condition for our existence.*
—SHOLEM ASCH

To live happily in a relationship we cannot repeatedly
dredge up the past, using it as a brickbat to pound
another human being into submission. Yet we all have
a tendency to do just that. "I told you so," and "You
should have listened when I gave you advice," and
"You were wrong" are phrases we may catch ourselves
uttering.

We can learn to give up that final piece of control,
that part which attempts to manipulate another human
being with guilt. We can't change another human being.
Our willingness to forgive errors, large and small, will
mark our own personal growth. Forgiveness is in our
own self-interest; we aren't free until we forgive.

*Today, I will let go of one grudge. As I grow
in understanding, I will grow in forgiveness.*

⌣ JUNE 16 ⌣

*We do not live an equal life, but one of contrasts
and patchwork; now a little joy, then a sorrow,
now a sin, then a generous or brave action.*
—Ralph Waldo Emerson

As our life experience unfolds, we live some days to the fullest and others in a very minimal way. If we focus too much on the less productive days or if we use them only as substandard comparisons to our best days, we may lose sight of the real value and meaning of the time we've been given.

A wholesome life, a productive life, a good life—whatever we call it—is not a shimmering length of perfectly woven cloth. It's more like a patchwork quilt set together by resourceful hands. We cannot choose to discard a bad experience or a poor decision; instead, we piece it into the total colorful work that is life.

*Today, I will be more aware of how the contrasts
of my life create a unique and beautiful pattern.*

⌒ JUNE 17 ⌒

Variety is the mother of enjoyment.
—BENJAMIN DISRAELI

Ideally, we anticipate awakening in the morning, not sure what the day is going to bring, but looking forward to it anyway. Sometimes this eagerness comes more easily, for we have places to go and people to see. At other times, we're unable to recapture our previous joy. What took away our excitement for life? What can we do to reclaim it?

Life does not end at retirement or when the children move away or when our good health is diminished. It just changes. We can develop some new interests and hobbies. We can reexamine old attitudes and come up with new perspectives. Music and good fellowship with others can enrich our lives and strengthen us to go on. We can turn to our spiritual natures, and we will know joy.

I am aware of the wonders and opportunities around me. I will share the joy I find.

∽ JUNE 18 ∽

Never believe in faith, see for yourself!
What you yourself don't learn, you don't know.
—BERTOLT BRECHT

While *faith* seems to be the watchword here, this quotation also extols the value of learning. Learning is not the opposite of faith. In fact, it supports and builds our faith. We often can trust our intuitions to guide us through all the lessons life provides us. It's up to us to pick and choose, to decide what lessons would be particularly pertinent to us, and to incorporate that knowledge into our own spirituality.

We learn firsthand, of course, from our own day-to-day lessons in living, but we also learn from the experiences of others, and these are equally beneficial to us. We can see for ourselves.

Learning strengthens my faith— in my Higher Power, in others, and in myself. I can use that greater faith to enhance and strengthen the quality of my life.

We can either change the complexities of life . . .
or develop ways that enable us to cope more effectively.
—HERBERT BENSON

Our illnesses have brought many new complexities into our lives, and our reactions may become much more intense as time goes on—especially if we feel helpless or pity ourselves.

All people have crises in their lives. Our medical conditions don't give us immunity from the normal problems, pains, and disappointments that all of us must face. If anything, we may have an advantage over people who have never had health problems; we have learned some coping skills in dealing with our medical conditions. Also, we have become more open to advice and support from others. We can be proud of how far we've come; we can be optimistic of how far we can go.

I will gladly exchange help
and support with my friends.

⌇ JUNE 20 ⌇

*Be content to grow a little each day. If the improvement
is the sort of thing which is very slow, do not measure
it too often. Do a self-comparison every two weeks,
or every six months— whatever is appropriate.*
—LEWIS F. PRESNALL

It's not easy to change the way our minds have been set,
but sometimes we really need to sit back and take stock
of how we have chosen to live—in both large and small
ways. We may realize that we are racing about without
so much as a moment for our own well-being. We
might even delude ourselves that we enjoy what we are
doing so much that it is for our well-being.

What matters most is that we vary the pace of our
days. We need the fast times, but the slower, easier
times are essential for our total health—emotional,
physical, social, and spiritual.

*I will slow down and spend
some quiet time with myself today.*

⮜ JUNE 21 ⮞

One cloud is enough to eclipse all the sun.
— THOMAS FULLER

Sometimes a beautiful day suddenly falls to pieces because of a criticism from a friend or being stuck in traffic before an important appointment. Later we may have wondered why one small happening could overshadow other happy events.

Quite possibly the answer lies within us and our expectations. If we expect each day and all our relationships to be without mishaps or misunderstandings, we set ourselves up to be disappointed. If we direct our energies toward pleasing our friends and relatives at the expense of our own needs and values, we are placing too much responsibility in their hands. We can have more rewarding days when our expectations are realistic. Each day will have unexpected delays or unappreciated remarks, but they are just a scattering of clouds in a bright, wide, wonderful sky.

I will have more realistic expectations.

⁓ JUNE 22 ⁓

Disability usually puts a strain on a good marriage
and exposes a bad one.
— ROBERT LOVERING

The strain on relationships of chronically ill people is
clearly shown in the fact that their divorce rate is higher
than the national average. Perhaps this is not so strange,
since any stressful situation only serves to point out any
preexisting deficits.

Suffering is a personal and lonely state even though
others have been where we are now. We can share some
of our pain with others. We can perhaps be an inspira-
tion to them because of how well we handle our suffering. We still can choose our attitudes and our responses.
Even though there are some situations we cannot control, there is always hope and help. We can receive relief
and understanding.

I will try to stay aware, in all my relationships,
of the added stresses caused by illness.

The degree and kind of sexuality of a human being
reaches up into the ultimate pinnacle of his spirit.
— FRIEDRICH NIETZSCHE

Having a long-term medical problem presents new problems, which we have to cope with as part of our total picture. One area that may present difficulties is sexuality.

Sexuality is how we think about ourselves, of how we present ourselves, of all that makes us unique. Our self-image may bottom out as we undergo the daily rigors of a medical problem, and we may for a time feel unsexual and unsensual. It takes us a while to realize that we still have the same needs we always had—to be touched and to feel good about ourselves. We don't have to be silent or passive. We need love and support, and sometimes we have to ask before our needs can be met.

I will remember that the quality of a relationship
depends on both people involved.

⌣ JUNE 24 ⌣

*There is a magnet in your heart that will
attract true friends. That magnet is unselfishness,
thinking of others first.*
—PARAMAHANSA YOGANANDA

Friendships develop slowly and are based on mutual interests and understanding. They are tested by time, by changes in life circumstances, and even by health. To be a real friend means being there when the chips are down, even when no one else is. It means giving and not receiving, but trusting that our friends are prepared to do the same.

Real friends take risks for one another—especially emotional risks—and still don't leave. A cherished friendship is not questioned, for we know, deep in our hearts, that we will always be there to help our close friends. We know they will always be there to help us.

*I have strong and rewarding relationships.
I cherish my friendships.*

⁓ JUNE 25 ⁓

Nothing is more fatal to health than an overcare of it.
— BENJAMIN FRANKLIN

Let's face it. There are certain times when we become preoccupied with our health. After all, if we'd broken a leg, we'd be abnormal if we weren't concerned with how we were going to walk or how frustrating it was. Long-term medical problems are a different matter. If we continue to constantly talk about our health, we will drive away the people we need most.

Talking less about our health problems may have benefits. We won't be wearing down our friends and family members with our lengthy medical discussions, and we also may become more accepting. To be alive is to experience challenges, problems, and conflicts. Acceptance ensures that we'll overcome some of the pain and that hope will be renewed.

Acceptance does bring relief and peace. God will grant me the serenity to accept the things I cannot change.

∼ JUNE 26 ∼

A man can't retire his experience. He must use it.
—BERNARD BARUCH

We may want to pretend that some of our life experiences didn't happen to us, but they did happen. We even helped create some of our bad experiences. We are the sum total of all those experiences.

We can own our behaviors and attitudes and even admit to the ones we are not comfortable with. By doing so, we are not permanently passing judgment on ourselves. We can use our negative experiences as a basis for the changes we need to make. Our weaknesses can be useful to us when we let them teach us where we need to begin our change. They will lead us to new attitudes and strengths we will be proud to claim as our own. When we are ready, we can create and accept improvements in ourselves.

I am the sum total of all my experiences. I can use my experiences to guide me into positive change.

⌒ JUNE 27 ⌒

The sky is not less blue
because the blind man does not see it.
—DANISH PROVERB

Each day we make our choices anew. We can choose to believe that pain and disappointment are the bitter fruits of living, or we can trust in our ability to build harmony, enthusiasm, and gratefulness from our day's experiences. We can hear the music of children's voices at play or be irritated at the disruption. We can pray, or we can chew on our anger.

We choose how we will see the world. If we feel anger and despair, if we hear only noise, if we see only dark, threatening clouds—that is our reality. But our negative choices don't change the world. Birds' songs and children's voices still fill the air. People still reach out to each other through love and caring. And the bright splash of sky is as blue as ever.

Today, my reality will be based on
the positive things around me.

～ JUNE 28 ～

Believe and remember this:
every saint and every sinner affects those whom he will
never see, because his words and deeds stamp themselves
upon the soft clay of human nature everywhere.
—JOSHUA LOTH LIEBMAN

In a world of billions of people, it's easy to feel insignificant. As a result, we might excuse ourselves for not acting upon our sense of rightness. After all, we might reason, what difference does it make? At those times, we've forgotten about the ripple effect.

Occasionally we've even seen our words and actions rippling from one person to another, but more often we see nothing at all. Then we must choose—whether to bitterly reject the idea of making a difference or to trust that someone, somewhere, is being comforted by a ripple of the wave we dared to make.

My presence is felt by people I know—
and by people I'll never know.

⸺ JUNE 29 ⸺

Give thanks for sorrow that teaches you pity;
for pain that teaches you courage— and give exceeding
thanks for the mystery which remains a mystery still—
the veil that hides you from the infinite, which makes it
possible for you to believe in what you cannot see.
—ROBERT NATHAN

We cannot run away from problems. Tremendous problems—like a spouse with a chronic illness—must be confronted and resolved. Fears can be overwhelming. Tasks seem endless, and the challenge seems too great. It is comforting to realize we face nothing alone.

We can't always be courageous, but fear is dispelled by our inner strength, by our trust that we will overcome problems and do as well as is possible. We can talk to ourselves in positive ways.

I will not allow fear and panic to overtake me today.
Courage will open the door to wisdom
and peace of mind.

⌣ JUNE 30 ⌣

The lame man who keeps the right road
outstrips the runner who takes a wrong one.
Nay, it is obvious that the more active and swift
the latter is the further he will go astray.
—FRANCIS BACON

As we travel through life, distractions keep us from reaching our destination. Sometimes a wonderful, happy circumstance changes our direction, or a goal may be changed by the intrusion of a serious medical condition.

Regardless of altered courses, we want to keep our goals in sight. We must set goals that, whatever our circumstances, we know are attainable. To feel successful and proud of ourselves, we must be able to attain our new goals. And we can if we aim toward ideals that provide dreams, challenges, and the possibility of success.

I follow the path that is best for me
and follow my own road map.

⌐ JULY 1 ⌐

Time flies . . . Time has wings . . .
Time and tide wait for no man.
— PROVERBS

We all have problems, but we deal with them in different ways. Some of us try to remove ourselves from the scene of our unhappiness. We get out of relationships, leave jobs, move away from our homes. Eventually, most of us realize that we have taken the major problems—ourselves and our behavior—with us. Time seems to crawl until we confront ourselves, decide to get help, and start to create change.

We need to make a true assessment of our problems. Then we can decide how willing we are to change those personal factors which contribute to the problems. Our load will begin to lighten, and time will once again have wings.

I recognize that my behavior dictates a large part
of my life. I am responsible for my own actions.

If I'd known I was going to live so long,
I'd have taken better care of myself.
— LEON ELDRED

We had few concerns when we were young other than eating, sleeping, and playing with friends. As we grew into young adulthood, we worked hard and played hard, often ignoring any signals our bodies gave us. We expected to be stiff after exercise, for example, and accepted it as part of our lifestyle.

By the time our chronic medical conditions became evident, our health habits were fairly well-established. We certainly can't undo the early care—or neglect—of our bodies. But we can learn new habits that will serve us well all the days of our lives.

Ultimately, my physical and emotional health depends
upon my willingness to take care of myself.

A chronic illness is a constant and sometimes overwhelming companion . . . only the power of a warm heart can alleviate the deep chill.
—Robert K. Massie

When our lifestyles change and an illness pervades our lives, we often feel lonely. It's not like a bad mood we can just shake off.

We need our friends and family around us, but it's up to us to give them the cue. People may stay at arm's length until we allow—even encourage—them to come closer. We need the support they can give us, and they need the satisfaction of contributing to our lives no matter how we've changed in our illness. We comfort and encourage each other, and we all feel blessed.

My illness has not changed the basic person I am. I needed the love and support of others before. I still do.

‿ JULY 4 ‿

Judge a tree from its fruit; not from the leaves.
—EURIPIDES

Sometimes we have a tendency to judge too quickly. Unfortunately, this is particularly true when we see people who are obviously physically impaired. We may form opinions of them based only on the fact that they walk differently or perhaps because they use a wheelchair.

We can judge people as individuals—not because of a medical condition. We can understand that people make their own individual marks on the world, not so much because of their physical abilities, but because of their mental and spiritual presence.

I will look beyond the external features of people and find the unique qualities within.

～ JULY 5 ～

When we do the best that we can, we never know what miracle is wrought in our life, or in the life of another!
—HELEN KELLER

When we toss a pebble into a pond, the widening concentric circles continue to spread—the ripple effect—long after the pebble is out of sight. Often the actions we take have similar results.

We don't always know what effect our lives and choices will have on other people. The immediate effects of our daily lives are probably easier to gauge, but often we don't see the long-term effect we have on others. And that really doesn't matter because all we are urged to do is to let kindness and responsibility rule our decisions. The immediate effect we see is the sense of growth within ourselves; the long-term effect we can trust to be a miracle that we may never see.

I'll remember that my actions affect many people beyond me.

~ JULY 6 ~

Yesterday is a cancelled check;
tomorrow is a promissory note;
today is the only cash you have — so spend it wisely.
— KAY LYONS

Each day is a small fragment of a lifetime. This fact frees us to focus on the things we truly can influence. We can never return to the past, except within our memories. And we don't know what the future holds in store. The only time we can "spend" is today; the only time we touch is right now.

The simplicity of the present allows us to let go of the past and to ignore the unknowns of the future. Thus freed, we can set about the business of enriching our lives physically, emotionally, and spiritually. Unpleasant debts to the past are paid, and we've mortgaged nothing to the future. We are free to invest in growth by using the "cash" we have on hand.

This day is a valuable piece of my life.
I will spend it well.

~ JULY 7 ~

Smiles form the channels of a future tear.
—LORD BYRON

We have often watched smiles turn to laughter and laughter back to tears. At a family reunion, we hear the joyous sounds of people chattering away, trying to catch up in five minutes for twenty lost years.

People who have Parkinson's disease sometimes complain that their faces don't match the emotions they want to express. The mask of the illness slows down normal movement of facial muscles. Even more tragic is the person who doesn't feel emotion. No laughter and no tears.

We are fortunate to be able to express our emotions, to show contentment and unhappiness. So what if today's laughter becomes tomorrow's tears? We know we'll laugh again—and cry again. Our past experiences give meaning to the present.

I will accept all my emotions as an affirmation of my life. Changing emotions are a part of normal living.

⌒ JULY 8 ⌒

They do me wrong who say I come no more,
For every day I stand outside your door.
—WALTER MALONE

Opportunity doesn't knock just once; it's there all the time. Perhaps we just don't see it because we're frightened to try new things. Or we may be complacent. One of the ways we know we are really making capable, mature decisions is when we become willing to open the door to opportunity again.

Occasionally, when a person retires, he or she may expect life to become automatically wonderful—all the time in the world and nothing in particular to do. It may take a little time for us to adjust. Opportunity is always there, waiting. We can learn to open our own doors.

I can renew my energies by becoming eager
to burst forward, to pursue leisure-time efforts,
to work with others.

~ JULY 9 ~

Should I, after tea and cakes and ices,
Have the strength to force the moment to its crisis?
—Thomas Stearns Eliot

Some people call it "dancing around the issue." After all, if there is a problem to face, we may become embarrassed when it's time to talk about it. We try so hard to balance the emotional framework of our lives that we hardly want to be the one to bring up what seems to be a taboo topic. What we think, we don't always state; what we intend, we don't state clearly; and what we need, we rarely ask for. Our half-truths and mixed messages don't result in honest communication.

Drug use? Manipulative behavior? Eating disorder? Financial problems? The only way to begin to face a problem is to admit that there is one, to talk about it, and to decide together what steps can be taken to help.

Today, I will face a problem honestly.

∽ JULY 10 ∽

It is costly wisdom that is bought by experience.
—ROGER ASCHAM

Wisdom is gained in many ways. We can learn from others, if we're willing. We can listen to the voice within—that inner sense of what can and should be done. Or we can—and quite often do—pay the price for that wisdom gained from experience.

Sometimes we ignore the cautioning voices of well-meaning friends and of our instincts and leap instead onto foolhardy or dangerous ground. It might have to do with family problems or finances or even our personal care. Often if we fail, we pay a great price—in terms of relationships, money, or health. But even our failures are not wasted if from them we gain the wisdom of caution and care.

*I will try to listen and learn from others
and thereby save myself some pain.*

~ JULY 11 ~

The biggest thing in our today's sorrow
is the memory of yesterday's joy.
—KAHLIL GIBRAN

Even though we intellectually know that a chronic illness will never go away, we emotionally offer ourselves a small glimmer of hope of recovery, of our lives going on as before.

We may spend some time reviewing life's memories, closing out whole chapters, and dealing with how life used to be. Then we can open a whole new section of life that allows us to include pain and sickness as part of our days. We work in the frame of reference of today. This is today's problem, and we can work it into our lives. Acknowledging that we are living a part of our lives differently from before will be our first step toward adjustment. We accept, we change, and we begin to create new joys in the present to ease our sorrow.

By offering my goals, I once again can move
into the mainstream of life.

∽ JULY 12 ∽

*There is a certain state of health
that does not allow us to understand everything;
and perhaps illness shuts us off from certain truths;
but health shuts us off just as effectively from others.*
—ANDRÉ GIDE

When we were healthy, it was hard imagining what someone in poor health was going through. We could sympathize—even empathize—but we were insulated from the reality because we had no personal experience with illness.

Now, our diminished health allows us to put ourselves in someone else's shoes. Many of our friends and family members don't always know how to act toward us or what to say. They're the ones who may be uneasy about facing our world. We can help them because we know what they are experiencing.

*I will be compassionate to my loved ones
as they strive to help and understand.*

⌁ JULY 13 ⌁

*We often make self-defeating choices
because we are unenlightened about our needs.
We pick the opposite of what we really need
because we don't know what we need.*
— LILA SWELL

Sometimes we may repeatedly engage in self-defeating behaviors. Poor work habits can lead to being fired and being defeated again. Overeating causes obesity, health issues, and poor image, which may lead to fad dieting and more failure. Until lightning strikes, until we finally realize that we are defeating our deepest needs—spiritual and emotional—we plod along on the same path.

The direction of our behavior changes when we see what our needs are and that they are the same for everyone. We all need love, compassion, and the opportunity to love others, and we can satisfy those needs in healthy ways.

I'll make positive choices for myself today.

Nothing is unthinkable, nothing impossible to the balanced person, provided it arises out of the needs of life and is dedicated to life's further developments.
—LEWIS MUMFORD

Occasionally, we may be discouraged over the loss of an ability we'd always counted on. Accepting this loss often requires a major emotional adjustment.

Our lives need not be defined by our inabilities, but instead by our possibilities. If bogged down in negativity, we may truly become the *dis*-abled people that others see at first glance.

Marvelous opportunities for growth and joy often await us—through doors we can choose to open and pass through. Almost nothing is impossible if we want to get there badly enough.

I won't use medical problems as excuses to bow out of life. Today, I will look for opportunities for challenge and growth.

~ JULY 15 ~

Let us then be up and doing, with a heart for any fate.
— Henry Wadsworth Longfellow

There may have been times in our lives when we were forced, for one reason or another, to eat a bland diet. The reasons don't matter; what does matter is how totally bored we became with the unvarying beige-and-white soft menu! Before long we had lost our anticipation of eating.

We may sometimes place ourselves on a bland diet of life. Daily routine stays much the same, day after day, year after year. From home to work to the sofa to bed, and start all over again. Some routine is like a healthy diet that gives us stability and safety, but a sprinkling of risk is the seasoning that adds zest to our lives. We can reach out for what is not habit. We can continue to try when previous efforts have failed. We can take a generous helping of life.

I can dare to change or to try new things without sacrificing all of my routine and safety.

~ JULY 16 ~

What is experience?
A poor little hut constructed from the ruins of the
palace of gold and marble called our illusion.
—JOSEPH ROUX

Our youthful dreams of glory, adventure, and wealth have, for most of us, been unfulfilled, yet we are not disappointed. Childlike illusions that a meaningful life has to be based on excitement and power have given way to a maturity that values simpler, yet more important, goals.

Our long-ago need for importance was based on the judgment of others. We wanted other people to see our wealth, feel our power, possibly even envy our influence. Today, we seek our own approval. We value serenity, not adventure. Love, not envy. Acceptance, not power. We live with goals, not illusions.

I am thankful that my values are strong.

A thing of beauty is a joy forever:
Its loveliness increases; it will never
Pass into nothingness.
—JOHN KEATS

We know a work of fine art can only increase in value. As the years pass by, art develops character lines which further define and highlight its beauty.

We wonder about people. There is grace that comes with age, we know, but how can people last forever? The answer, of course, is we do not. But all that we comprise and create—the love, the caring, the storytelling, the things we make with our hands—will endure forever. Just as enduring, and perhaps even more valuable, is the respect we give to our families and traditions. These and other family heirlooms are our assurance that no one or no thing passes into nothingness.

I am comforted by the traditions of family and faith and by the meaningfulness they add to my life.

⟿ JULY 18 ⟿

Who controls the past controls the future;
who controls the present controls the past.
—GEORGE ORWELL

We planned on being healthy, on always being healthy, so our adjustment to less-than-optimal health can be quite difficult. Until we get our priorities back in gear, it can seem as though the scales are just not tipping in our favor.

Life can feel overwhelming when we foresee no apparent reprieve from our pain and inconvenience. It takes a while sometimes to learn to live with a health problem, but we can do it. With time we gain insight. Our lives are in our control once again.

We are responsible for ourselves, although sometimes we may forget that fact. Once we get a firm hold on our emotions, on our new set of problems, we understand that we still make the decisions for ourselves.

I can make positive decisions that
alter the path of my life.

Our faith comes in moments; our vice is habitual.
—RALPH WALDO EMERSON

Some habits are not good for us, yet we can fall into them so easily. "Just one more drink," we rationalize. "It won't hurt me. I don't have to go to work tomorrow." "Just a small piece of cake. I'll start my diet tomorrow." We may not realize that we are acting in a pattern. Being human, we continue in this way until something happens that forces us to change our patterns and ourselves.

Whatever that something is, it may prompt many actions, one of which may be to turn to our faith for solace. Many things in our lives are uncertain. There is uncertainty as to how our day will be. It is our faith that keeps us going regardless of any setbacks. The moments of darkness we all fall into can be overcome by faith.

I can believe and trust in my Higher Power
no matter what is happening in my life now.

*We should not let our fears hold us back
from pursuing our hopes.*
—JOHN F. KENNEDY

Regardless of our situation, we all need to hope. When we were young, we were in a hurry all the time. Every problem needed a quick solution. And our antici- pated futures were completely untarnished by adult viewpoints.

Sometimes, what we mislabel as a fear of dying might really be regret that we haven't led a full enough life. We know now what is reasonable and what is not. We understand where we are in our lives and accept that ideal situations may not come to pass. We have learned that we must come to terms with who we are and what we can do. We have learned that we are okay just as we are today.

*I have come to terms with where I am in my life.
My fears will not hold me back anymore.*

An hour of pain is as long as a day of pleasure.
— PROVERB

When we look back at our lives, do the painful experiences come through first? We may remember the difficult times that led to the end of a relationship or the loss of a job. Life seemed at a standstill during those times, as we wondered whether we'd ever get close to another person, find another job, or feel confident again.

We probably learned much later that failures could be opportunities for growth. As we sift through our hardest memories, we can settle back into the happy ones again, knowing we have learned and grown from our pain. And as our "hour" of pain comes to an end, we can see the large and small pleasures of today and remember those of yesterday.

I will not let pain obscure my joys and pleasures.

*We must believe in the conquest of the spirit of
the world by the spirit of God. But, the miracle must
happen in us, before it can happen in the world.*
—ALBERT SCHWEITZER

There is a time in the progression of life or pain or illness when we realize that no matter how extensive our resources are, no matter how deep our emotional well, we cannot depend only upon ourselves. We all recognize that time when it's at hand; no one has to inform us.

Even if our faith has been shaken before, we are able, once again, to reach out to a Power greater than ourselves. Our Higher Power offers reassurance that even as we continue to adjust, even when we have coped as well as we can, a greater comfort and care is open to us.

*I can't control everything.
I find freedom and relief in knowing I don't have to.*

∼ JULY 23 ∼

A friend is clearer than the light of heaven,
for it would be better for us that the sun were
extinguished than that we should be without friends.
—St. John Chrysostom

Friendship is our greatest achievement and reward. Our friends are people to care about, celebrate with, and count on. Even after the diagnosis of a chronic medical condition, friends are there for each other. Within the closest friendships we find the best of each other at all times.

Friendships enrich our lives. It is no accident that we become close and maintain our contact. Our paths crossed for reasons, and we are forever a part of each other's life. We really listen. We open up. We offer help and hope. We share each other's pain and enhance each other's growth. We appreciate our friend's unique qualities. We let each other know who we really are.

I bring myself honestly to my friendships.

*Keep your fears to yourself
but share your courage with others.*
—ROBERT LOUIS STEVENSON

Each of us harbors secret fears. "How will I manage?" "Can I make it through today?" "Will my family still love me if my behavior has been inappropriate?"

We learn, rather early in the game, that a defeatist attitude drives our friends away after a period of time. Therefore, it's often up to us to deal with our own fears. We do our best to ease ourselves through each crisis— and at times we will need additional help—but by and large we can do it. It isn't so much that we're overly independent or angry. It's that we need to help our loved ones learn how to cope with our illnesses, so we do our best to keep our fears from becoming irrational. And that often passes for courage.

*I will put my fears into proper perspective
because this helps me— and my loved ones.*

~ JULY 25 ~

He who knows others is learned,
He who knows himself is wise.
—Lao Tsze

We sometimes let how we think we should act keep us from showing our deepest feelings. We may behave the way others expect us to act, while burying within ourselves the pain and fears associated with our changing health.

Acting upon our own thoughts and feelings can be difficult; acting according to what others think is frustrating—and impossible. Gradually we find more stability and confidence within ourselves. This self-trust allows us to show our emotions and to express our ideas and feelings. We might be short-tempered sometimes, or impatient, or angry. None of us is perfect. We accept that truth and are freed of the burden of pleasing others; we discover the joy of acting on our inner messages of growth and honesty.

I am most free to grow when I am
acting honestly on my own values and feelings.

The future is called "perhaps," which is
the only possible thing to call the future.
And the important thing is not to allow that to scare you.
— TENNESSEE WILLIAMS

"I'm going to work in the mills, like my dad." "I'm going to be a teacher." "I want to be a soldier." As children, we believed in these absolute, fixed goals. In adulthood, we learn that we don't always get what we expect. Sometimes we don't even come close. Those who manage to live happy and fulfilling lives are flexible, mature adults.

Flexibility means we can incorporate changes into our lives, even when those changes cause a difference in the way we live. What's most important is to remember that we can change goals and attain them, that happiness is there if we work and plan for it.

I am not afraid to make changes that are good for me.

*One of the signs of maturity is a healthy respect
for reality— a respect that manifests itself in
the level of one's aspirations and in the accuracy of
one's assessment of the difficulties which separate the
facts of today from the bright hopes of tomorrow.*
—ROBERT H. DAVIES

If we don't want to live our lives caught in the "what might have been" doldrums, we can assess where we are and how we happen to be here. We can stop feeling regretful about lost time and concentrate on the possibilities now.

If we haven't achieved any of the goals we previously set for ourselves, we can make new goals and achieve each of them one step at a time. We have the rest of our lives to live, and we can realistically shape new goals that are both challenging and reachable.

*I will set realistic goals,
realizing there is never a better time than now.*

⌣ JULY 28 ⌣

Life is not a "brief candle." It is a splendid torch
that I want to make burn as brightly as possible
before handing it on to future generations.
—George Bernard Shaw

How lucky we are to have the splendid torch of our
lives shining on our days. Some may think that a health
problem is going to become a permanent barrier to our
ability to enjoy life.

If we assume that each one of our "small candles"
represents another of our strengths, we can blend them
together to form a torch of hope. How we live the rest of
our lives—forty months or forty years—is entirely our
own making. Let the torch shine!

The possibilities of my life are endless
when I am willing to see them and act on them.

Positive attitudes — optimism, high self-esteem, and outgoing nature, joyousness, and the ability to cope with stress — when established early in life, may be the most important basis for continued good health.
—HELEN HAYES

Positive attitudes and high self-esteem are wonderful attributes, but not all of us are lucky enough to develop them early in our lives. Because we haven't developed strong coping strategies doesn't mean we don't have the opportunity now. It's hard to change, and we can only do it if it becomes important for us to make the effort.

When we are going through stressful times, especially those times related to a health problem, we can develop our courage by acting "as if" we have high self-esteem, "as if" we can cope well. Remarkably, we may find that we do.

A time of high stress has forced me to face my own character deficits. I am working on developing positive attitudes.

～ JULY 30 ～

*There is nothing which we receive
with so much reluctance as advice.*
—JOSEPH ADDISON

As children, most of us were unreceptive to advice. Our parents offered words of warning, and frequently we refused to hear because we needed independence.

Today, when friends or family members make suggestions, we might have some of the same reactions as we did as children. We still need independence, and some advice—no matter how well meant—carries with it the implication that we are less than capable of clearly seeing dangers or knowing our options. We're better able now to weigh the messages we receive. We have two choices. When our loved ones offer suggestions that we know to be bad or inappropriate for us, we can remind ourselves that they are meant well and merely say thank you. When the advice is good, we can do the same thing.

I will listen carefully to all the loving advice given me.

～ JULY 31 ～

From happiness to suffering is a step;
from suffering to happiness is an eternity.
—JEWISH PROVERB

The loss of normal good health can rock even the strongest person. In one fragile moment our lives seem in shambles. All that we anticipated, all that we had planned, seems over forever. We wonder if we'll ever get through this suffering.

For a while it may seem as though we are living underwater—nothing is clear or straightforward. The things that once gave us pleasure seem to disappear as grief takes their place. Friends offer to help—and they do help for a time—but ultimately we face our loss alone.

Finally we begin to understand that grief is a process, just as life is a process. We will be able to move toward acceptance and serenity, and eventually we can be happy again. We can continue to live.

I am consoled in knowing grief takes time,
but it will end. I can continue to grow.

⚬ AUGUST 1 ⚬

Oft when the white still dawn
Lifted the skies
and pushed the hills apart
I have felt it like glory in my heart.
—EDWIN MARKHAM

The world is one, a whole, and we are a part of it. But sometimes, we are so enmeshed in ourselves—in the details of our lives, in the unfair limitations placed upon us—that we become closed and forget the rest of the world. We see nothing else. We hear nothing else.

But if we reenter the world, the natural balance there gives us peace and comfort. The beauty—splashes of color, fragrance of flowers, trees swaying in a breeze—is also our beauty. We inhale the breath of spring amid the sounds of life. All seems right with the world, and we are one with all life.

Today, I will find joy and meaning
in being alive within a living world.

~ AUGUST 2 ~

No man is good for anything who has not some particle of obstinacy to use upon occasion.
—HENRY WARD BEECHER

The word *obstinate* is quite often used to describe children who refuse to let go of an idea or behavior. Although we may not want others to label us obstinate, it might be that obstinacy is a needed quality for us in the right situations.

Sometimes it is healthy for us to be stubborn, to hold steadfastly to what we want and who we are and where we want to be. Faith in ourselves and obstinacy can be just what we need to survive a hard day. And we do get by, not because we're foolish, but because our maturity tells us to hold on to our sense of direction.

I will keep as much independence as I can.

~ AUGUST 3 ~

*Somewhere along the line of development
we discover what we really are, and then we make our
real decision for which we are responsible.*
— ELEANOR ROOSEVELT

Many of us have begun to reexamine our lives and our values. Am I proud of how I act? Of what I do? Will this decision be in my best interest? Do I have strong, interacting relationships?

A likely result of this examination might be that we fool ourselves less now and that we don't try to fool others. The discovery of what we really are and of what is important to us urges us toward greater honesty. We are freer to make amends to friends and family members for things we've said or done. We hesitate less in asking for help and in telling others when we feel wronged. Best of all, we've rid ourselves of our old victim mentality and have taken responsibility for our lives.

I will begin happily to make responsible decisions today.

~ AUGUST 4 ~

*Today is the day in which to express your noblest
qualities of mind and heart, to do at least one worthy
thing which you have long postponed. . . .*
— GRENVILLE KLEISER

Volunteer work. There are volunteer jobs for people
with every level of ability. The main qualification is to
care about others. Each day offers us the opportunity to
make a difference in someone else's life. We may choose
to sing in a community choir or to play in an amateur
band. Or we might offer to read stories to or write letters for people with limited vision.

Volunteer work. What's remarkable are the benefits
we will reap from the simple act of sharing our abilities,
our lives, our caring. These acts affirm the bond that
exists between us. They help us move out of a preoccupation with ourselves and our limitations, and they put
us into the mainstream of life.

Today, I will share my abilities and talents with others.

*My handicap is part of me because I have had to
make peace with it. And in doing so, I've made
peace with the less obvious handicaps of other people,
like resentment, prejudice, hate.*
—GINGER HUTTON

Living with an illness—whether our own or a loved
one's—has taught us that handicaps are not always
physical. We begin to understand that fear is handicapping, prejudice is handicapping, inaccessibility to the
community is handicapping.

More and more we are able to make peace with our
own limitations and those of others, and as we do this
we gain insight into which of them we have to accept
and which we don't. We recognize there are some limitations we can do something about and others we must
accept for the sake of our serenity.

The more tolerant I am, the less limited I become.

*Believe, when you are most unhappy, that there is
something for you to do in the world. So long as you
can sweeten another's pain, life is not in vain.*
—HELEN KELLER

Day-to-day problems can become so overwhelming that
we just can't fathom how we will manage. At those
times, the three most difficult things to do might be the
very things we should do.

First, we must admit to ourselves that we are, indeed, in an emotional crisis. Then, we should reach out
to the community for support. People never know we
need help if we don't ask. A nearly endless array of services is in place for us—grief groups, counseling,
Alcoholics Anonymous, Al-Anon, Overeaters Anonymous, and other Twelve Step groups. Third, we have
the option of moving beyond ourselves and reaching
out to someone else who suffers.

*It's within my power to help myself by
connecting with people who care.*

～ AUGUST 7 ～

Eat little at night, open your windows, drive out often,
and look for the good in things and people. . . .
You will no longer be sad, or bored, or ill.
—MARY KNOWLES

When we get caught up in our problems, it may seem that they will continue to escalate, repeat, and escalate again. We all have hard times—times when we are uncertain whether or not life has meaning, and at those times it may feel as though we have no control over the direction or quality of our lives.

But when we ease back a little and remember the hundreds of small choices we can make, we're more able to accept some of the large, unchangeable realities of our lives. We can't cure ourselves or change other people, but we can make the choices and take charge of the decisions that are ours.

I can simplify my life by letting go of decisions
and problems that aren't mine to handle.

⸻ AUGUST 8 ⸻

Man can do much for himself as respects his own improvement, unless self-love so blinds him that he cannot see his own imperfections and weaknesses.
— MARTHA WILSON

Remember hide-and-seek? Oleeey oleeey in free? What wonderful times they were when we were so certain we could hide from others. Now we are adults, and one would think we are no longer hiding. That's not, unfortunately, always true. Many of us hide within negative behaviors that become habits.

Looking at our own weaknesses is a difficult task. We understand we have character defects, but we're afraid to change our familiar patterns. If we can admit there is a problem, we've taken the first step. Wanting to change comes next. Finally, we won't be hiding anymore.

*Self-improvement is within my reach
if I admit my negative behavior.*

Usually when people are sad, they don't do anything.
They just cry over their condition. But when they
get angry, they bring about a change.
—MALCOLM X

Those of us who have a chronic illness often feel a lot of anger, but we can choose how to deal with the anger. If we insist on denying it, we may isolate ourselves and be numbed by an unbearable sadness. Or we might lash out at the people we love.

A sounder choice for us is to acknowledge our anger—and our right to be angry. We don't deserve illness. Or pain. When we allow ourselves these honest reactions, we are freer to move toward acceptance—and action. When we accept our limitations—no matter how unfair they are—we then can decide where and how and when we will make needed changes in our lives.

My anger can lead me toward growth
if I use it in the right ways.

～ AUGUST 10 ～

Few men are so miserable as
not to like to talk of their misfortunes. . . .
—MARIA EDGEWORTH

"Don't get stuck in a conversation with Harry. He'll bore you to death telling you his problems." We have all had the experience of being warned away from a certain person. There have probably even been times when we were the "Harry" others tried to avoid. It's normal to dwell on our troubles, and we all like to talk about them. There is an added responsibility on our shoulders now that there is a medical problem present.

We can minimize that problem by becoming aware of what we are doing and by saving our long medical conversations for the people who really care and need to know. Otherwise, we will find that our friends will slip away, uncertain of how to bear the burden of our changed health.

Caution *will become my watchword as*
I learn to live with my altered health patterns.

⌒ AUGUST 11 ⌒

Before an important decision someone clutches
your hand—a glimpse of gold in the iron-gray,
the proof of all you have never dared to believe.
—DAG HAMMARSKJÖLD

There is nothing quite as lonely as having to make a decision. Imagine the feelings a family goes through when a beloved pet has to be put to sleep. The parents, because they truly understand the situation, must be the decision makers. If we are considering a job change, it will affect our immediate family and our friendships.

When a person extends a helping hand, we welcome it as a starving person would welcome food, for it offers affirmation and empathy. The decision is still difficult, but we have the inner strength to carry us through.

I believe in myself, but will welcome the
support of others in my decision making.

Life is so full of miseries, minor and major. . . .
—AGNES REPPLIER

Occasionally, a person who has chronic pain spends far too much time on a quest to cure or solve the pain. Support groups become much more than an extension of helpful purpose; they can become our total purpose. All the day can be filled with seeking the "right" people to solve our problems. All semblance of a well-balanced life gets pushed away.

There's no reason to make our days miserable with unrealistic goals. Learning to live the best we can with the pain and inconvenience of illness is the only way to make minor miseries out of major ones.

I can keep myself emotionally whole
by seeking balance in my life.

If you allow men to use you for your own purposes,
they will use you for theirs.
—AESOP

When we attend a party, isn't it always the person with the cast or someone who just had surgery who gets all the attention? At first, when our health changes, we may try to play other people for sympathy.

We finally begin to understand that most of us have different needs. Ours are more permanent than the needs of a person with a broken leg. Upon realizing this, we could become angry that our needs aren't being anticipated. After being ill for a while, we realize it's up to us to let others know what we are feeling and what our needs are. Then we can look for understanding, not pity.

Exploiting the role of "sick person"
is one behavior I need to guard against.
I will accept this as a personal challenge.

⌒ AUGUST 14 ⌒

Physical strength can never permanently
withstand the impact of spiritual force.
—Franklin Delano Roosevelt

It's a peculiar twist of life that physical impairment causes some of us to become either agnostic or more spiritual. Few of us stay in the shades of gray.

Those of us who are fortunate enough to find our Higher Power or to rediscover our sense of spirituality may feel a deep and abiding belief in spiritual forces that will dwell with us at all times in our lives.

Spirituality transcends all health problems; we can call on its comfort and support at will. Our beliefs can buoy us up when we are feeling low and can richly enhance all the facets of our lives.

The spiritual forces that work within me
are uniquely mine— to share or to keep private.
They will always enhance my life.

∼ AUGUST 15 ∼

As we advance in life,
we learn the limits of our abilities.
—J. A. FROUD

Remember the lofty goals we had when we were young? Goals that included being the best, saving all the children, having a lot of money. We could be president, put out fires, or be on stage. We could accomplish anything when we were young. The older we got, the more realistic we became. We began to be aware of what we couldn't do, of the fact that not every family system worked, that not every person was happy.

We found new goals then, goals that we could live with for that time in our lives. Even now, as we read, we are learning about ourselves. We know that we may not reach our childhood goals. We have learned our limits and are living our lives in a realistic fashion.

Awareness of my own limits has helped me
set realistic goals. I am successful.

Be not afraid of life. Believe that life is worth living
and your belief will help create the fact.
— WILLIAM JAMES

The words *life is worth living* may seem inappropriate to someone who has a serious personal conflict. A pat on the shoulder or a hug just isn't enough to convince us that all we are going through makes life "worth living."

A sense of worthiness is an ongoing process. And the value of life is affirmed and strengthened by our willingness to listen to our emotional and physical needs—especially when we feel unhappy or unhealthy. That willingness is shown in action. A cup of coffee and a good cry with a close friend, acceptance of our Higher Power's wisdom and care, or seeking help from a trained professional—all of these actions say, "I and my life have worth."

By helping myself, I will act on
my belief that life is worth living.

～ AUGUST 17 ～

Sadness is almost never anything but a form of fatigue.
—ANDRÉ GIDE

There are times in every life when the road gets a little bumpy. Occasionally we become so overwhelmed with work, with life in general, that we become exhausted. With the fatigue can come sadness—sadness at not being able to work the way we expected to, sadness at not looking or feeling as well as we want to, or sadness caused by grieving. We may feel sorry for ourselves or feel nearly paralyzed by fatigue.

We can recognize that fatigue is one of the many forms that sadness takes. Feelings of sorrow or helplessness can be diminished by confiding them to a friend or to a physician. We can only be as well as we expect to be—as well as we allow ourselves to be.

When I feel very fatigued or sad,
I can be open and honest about my problem.
Hiding behind fatigue only causes sadness.

⤸ AUGUST 18 ⤹

*You may judge others only according
to your knowledge of yourself.*
— Kahlil Gibran

We know that our behavior patterns may not be the only acceptable ones. Many of us have spent the major part of our lives trying to please others. Now we are learning to please ourselves. We finally understand that there's no need for us to reach beyond our own capabilities.

Now that our physical health is limited and our emotional health is stretched almost to the breaking point, we begin to realize that people around us may have serious problems of their own. By reaching out, unselfishly, we can help. Inadvertently, we will reap the benefits of our own behavior.

*As I understand my limitations,
I begin to know myself more intimately than ever before.
I am learning about my untapped potential.*

～ AUGUST 19 ～

*The past should be culled like a box of fresh
strawberries, rinsed of debris, sweetened judiciously
and served in small portions, not very often.*
—LAURA PALMER

Many of us may dwell in the past, telling ourselves our yesterdays were better than our tomorrows will ever be. Living in "what was" can be dangerous, for we may be less adaptable to life's changes.

Fond memories are healthy when they remind us how our lives are formed and shaped by our experiences. Memories reveal our development into the productive people we are today. Life does get better every day because we have both the joys of the present and some sweet memories of the past. We not only survive, we regain happiness and our peace of mind by living for today and by appreciating all the todays and yesterdays.

*I will not live in the past, but instead will look
to each day as new and promising.*

~ AUGUST 20 ~

Repose is not more welcome to the worn and to the aged,
to the sick and to the unhappy, than danger, difficulty,
and toil, to the young and the adventurous.
—FANNY BURNEY

Within the same week, a ten-year-old boy made a solo
flight across America, and a woman who was over eighty
climbed Mount Everest. Some of us don't aspire to such
mind-boggling events. But there is a time for more adventurous quests and a time for quiet. They don't have
to be age-related.

Sometimes our concern about age may be more limiting than our physical capabilities. "Should a person
my age be acting like this?" "I think I'm too old for that."
Thoughts like these prevent us from exploring and
learning and acquiring new skills. We can choose our
direction, regardless of age.

I will set aside age prejudice when
I look at the possibilities before me today.

Nothing can bring you peace but yourself.
— RALPH WALDO EMERSON

True peace comes from the harmony we feel within ourselves. We don't go out and get peace of mind; it's the result of what we do. Harmony is being at ease with ourselves, our surroundings, and our lives. This is no easy task, as we must come to grips with the issues that cause us concern.

This doesn't mean that all our problems must be solved before we can have inner peace, for life will be much like a mountain road, with twists and turns and many unexpected bumps. Peace is a reality for those who accept what cannot be changed and take up the challenges that can and must be dealt with. Peace is easier to attain when we cherish the gifts of the present moment.

In my life, peace begins with me.
I will remember that peace is a prize of the spirit
and is available to everyone.

I have gout, asthma, and seven other maladies,
but am otherwise very well.
— SYDNEY SMITH

We may be awed by people who are able to handle any problem that comes their way. They seem to have a magic touch. They are strong, we think, and they seem to so easily separate their emotional and spiritual selves from what happens to them physically.

There are people who can always manage to find happiness. Indeed, they often can find laughter in the midst of chaos. We may feel jealous of their apparent ability to handle troubles. Often, however, we learn that they have come through terrible life crises, abusive relationships, bouts with cancer, or chronic health difficulties. The ones we envy may have learned, the hard way, that each problem must be handled on its merit. There is no magic touch, just touching experiences.

I may have problems, but I can allow myself
the right to be otherwise well.

So never let a cloudy day ruin your sunshine,
for even if you can't see it, the sunshine is still there,
inside of you, ready to shine when you will let it.
—AMY MICHELLE PITZELE

Amazing words of wisdom sometimes spring from the mouths of children. This child was just nine years old when she wrote these words, which are the last stanza of a poem about understanding change. Life seen through the eyes of a child can be serenely simplistic. Where does a child get that kind of wisdom and that depth of understanding?

We can struggle to keep the child in us alive. We, too, can recognize that even when the cloudy days come, the sunshine—our smiles, our hopes, our dreams—is still there, ready to beam at a moment's notice.

Today, my own personal sun will shine within me,
no matter what the weather is outside.

～ AUGUST 24 ～

Faults are thick where love is thin.
— JAMES HOWELL

We often overlook the faults of people we love. Sometimes, in fact, our love so blinds us that we don't have to overlook their faults, because we don't even see them. Yet if our love wavers or if a friendship begins to weaken, it may seem as though our friends have developed numerous flaws or maddening habits.

When this happens, we learn to reassess our relationship and ourselves. Rather than conclude that our loved one has become less than he or she was before, we know that change has occurred within us. Then we decide whether the friendship is important enough to try to rebuild it. Sometimes it is, and we work to recapture the trust and communication we once had. Sometimes it isn't, and we decide to let go of it and, in doing so, let go of resentment and fault-finding.

The decision to rebuild or to let go of
friendships often rests with me.

~ AUGUST 25 ~

*Sometimes it is more important to discover
what one cannot do, than what one can do.*
— LIN YUTANG

Understanding limitations is important in our lives. As we mature, we naturally let go of old dreams and develop new ones. We start to reexamine, to set priorities, to find out what we are capable of and what we are still able to accomplish. Finally, we understand that we may not be the tallest, the richest, the handsomest, or the most intelligent.

We learn how to find what is normal for us, how to establish a new balance in our lives. We learn to accept who we are. Acceptance of change in our lives includes those changes which occur with chronic health problems. This is one of our most difficult challenges, but we will grow in our ability to cope with this illness too.

*I continually struggle to find the new balance in my life,
but I know it's a growth process of which I'm capable.*

*Friendship: A ship big enough to carry
two in fair weather, but only one in foul.*
—AMBROSE BIERCE

Let's be honest. When we have choice, don't we avoid aggravation, fear, and pain in our friendships? Before we judge friends and family members who have been unable to cope with our chronic conditions, we should ask ourselves to understand their choice. Certainly, we wouldn't choose to have the pain, inconvenience, and limitations of our illnesses if we had the same choice as they do.

Most of us have been hurt by friends who have abandoned us because of our medical conditions, but it might be time now for us to forgive them. We can remind ourselves that abandonment does not mean our friends were unloving or uncaring; it only means they selected an option that we don't have.

I will work to forgive those who have left me.

The essence of optimism is that it . . . enables a man to hold his head high, to claim the future for himself and not abandon it to his enemy.
—DIETRICH BONHOEFFER

"She always looks to the sour side," we've heard it said, or, "He always has a pleasant smile." The difference, as we all know, between an optimist and a pessimist is entirely in their attitudes. A pessimist sees little, if anything, to look forward to in life. In that case, life is tediously lived. If we think in positive ways, we see the good. That good becomes the primary part of our lives.

An optimist, regardless of personal problems, is eager to arise in the morning—to get to work, to be with friends or family, to live the happiness of the day. People are drawn toward optimists, for their joy shines on everyone around them.

Life is an adventure of choices to be lived, not an ordeal to be survived. I choose optimism and joy.

～ AUGUST 28 ～

Pain is life — the sharper, the more evidence of life.
— CHARLES LAMB

We all have pain in our lives. This is not necessarily illness, but deeper emotional pain caused by our perception of failure or success. Caused by a relationship ending. Caused by loss. Caused by giving up unrealistic goals. We all experience pain.

We gain the knowledge that pain broadens our base of experience and can make us stronger—or weaker. And we are the ones who ultimately have to carry the burden and joy of our lives.

There's more here than "pain in life." It's how we learn to handle our pain, how we react to what has caused our pain, and how we have made others feel about our pain that matters the most.

I choose to be a survivor.
My experiences can enrich my life.

Lord, teach us to number our days,
that we may apply our hearts unto wisdom.
—Psalm 90

Funny, but when we were kids, we probably didn't give much thought to words such as *peace* and *harmony*. We just lived our sweet childish lives with little, if any, worry about feelings.

Now we speak often of "meeting of the minds," "harmonious thoughts," and "world peace," for we all want to achieve as high a level of personal and emotional comfort as we are able. With our newly developed understanding of wisdom comes a deepened sense of pride because we know that each day is a precious entity, special in and of itself.

The harmony and peace that surround me
are mine for the taking.

*The basic fact of today is the
tremendous pace of change in human life.*
—Jawaharlal Nehru

Just when we convince ourselves that we are settled, something happens that causes us to change once again. We need to become chameleons, open to change and willing to adapt.

It's not a simple process, for sometimes life throws us zingers we never expected. Not all change is positive, and it can be downright hard. Perhaps we may become grandparents quite unexpectedly, or we may need to move to a different city. We can lose a spouse or a job or our health. All these situations cause further change. Rising to the occasion teaches us that we are, finally, truly adult in our behavior.

*I let go of old dreams each time I change.
I am proud of my ability to adapt to new circumstances.*

A mature person is one who does not think only in absolutes, who is able to be objective even when deeply stirred emotionally. . . .
—ELEANOR ROOSEVELT

Many of us are well aware of how easily tempers flare or tears can flow when we face an unexpected problem or situation. Perhaps illness contributes to this sensitivity, but we might also consider whether we've become more rigid. Are we holding too tightly to absolutes, wanting to have the right answer or the right response to almost everything? Has coping with unpredictable illnesses driven us to seek predictability in other areas of our lives?

Maturity often means letting go of the need to control. We also find greater peace by allowing ourselves to be unprepared for people and events we can't prepare for. There are no absolutes, and we don't have to live as though there were.

I will be willing to consider new ideas.

∼ SEPTEMBER 1 ∼

*Spirituality is like a bird: if you hold on to it tightly,
it chokes, and if you hold it loosely, it escapes.*
— ISRAEL SALANTER LIPKIN

Being spiritual does not necessarily mean being religious. Instead, it can be an awakening of our deepest personal sense of caring about other people, as well as an awakening of our appreciation of the joy, symmetry, and balance of nature.

The spirituality we strive for and which comforts us best is based on our finding a similar balance within ourselves. When we possessively clutch our faith and expect all that we demand, our spirituality is weakened. Yet, if we expect nothing of it, it might seem to disappear. Our spiritual lives are strengthened as we find that precious balance between expectant trust in our Higher Power and responsible reliance on ourselves.

*I am striving to find fullness and balance in my days.
Certain experiences change the balance,
but I can find it again.*

∽ SEPTEMBER 2 ∽

My coat and I live comfortably together.
It has assumed all my wrinkles, does not hurt me
anywhere, has molded itself on my deformities,
and is complacent to all my movements.
I only feel its presence because it keeps me warm.
—VICTOR HUGO

The anticipation of school beginning each fall is fueled by youngsters' love of newness—new clothes, new shoes, new books, new teachers. We still enjoy newness, but we also find comfort in what is old and reliable. No afghan comforts quite as well as the one that was knitted with loving hands many years ago. We may have a favorite mug or chair. Over the years we have developed trusting and dependable relationships. While we remain open to change, we also feel comfortable with what is old and familiar.

I'm glad I can find comfort in the old and familiar,
and excitement in the new and unfamiliar.

My message is peace of mind,
not curing cancer, blindness, or paraplegia. . . .
Anyone who is willing to work at it can achieve it.
—BERNIE S. SIEGEL

Too often, we think we can regain our peace of mind only after our health problems are resolved. But peace of mind is what we need right now, not later. We can do a few things in our medical treatment, but we can actively develop our spiritual and emotional strengths.

We can look at life not in terms of success or failure, but in terms of attitudes and beliefs and self-acceptance. We can reprioritize our life goals to emphasize what can be done. Gradually, we experience a sense of peace as we separate those things we can change and control from those we cannot. Making our choices and acting upon them brings us the peace we need in difficult times.

I will consider only the choices
that are truly mine to make.

*I learned that nothing is impossible
when we follow our inner guidance,
even when its direction may threaten us
by reversing our usual logic.*
—GERALD G. JAMPOLSKY

Two voices play about our heads. We hear, "Do it the way you've always done it," and the opposing, "Take a chance—you can do it a different way." Sometimes we have to take a chance—on ourselves, on finding a better way.

What if we walk a new, longer, less convenient path home? What if we abandon the unsuccessful patterns we've followed with our loved ones? What if we speak our minds, rather than remain silent? Good things can happen when we dare to change. And if nothing happens? We would still have the pleasure of a new way home, of communicating on a different level, of knowing the joy of daring to change.

*When I follow my inner voice,
my opportunities are endless.*

No faith is our own that we have not arduously won.
—HAVELOCK ELLIS

Everything that touches our lives influences our level of trust and spirituality. There are times when our faith, especially in ourselves, goes astray. This may be caused by losing a job, losing our good health, or enduring a negative change in a relationship. Our faith can be shaken when the things we expected to always be there are suddenly gone.

We can begin to regain that faith by remembering our Higher Power is constant, even when our faith is not. We humans fluctuate between doubt and trust, but that doesn't diminish the care that is always available to us. We need only surrender to that truth, and we find comfort.

My faith—in myself and in my Higher Power— is built upon my awareness that I don't have to struggle alone. I am strengthened when I admit to my spiritual needs.

Lie down and listen to the crabgrass grow,
the faucet leak, and learn to leave them so.
— MARYA MANNES

Sometimes we are driven by a need to get everything done. We have an inner sense of what we should be, and we work toward meeting that expectation. But we may strive beyond those goals because of what we believe our friends, our co-workers, and even the advertising media expect of us.

Only we can decide which expectations to satisfy. But first, we must be sure that the things we strive for are really our needs and goals. If an alphabetized spice rack or an organized workbench gives us no satisfaction, why should we alphabetize or organize? If an imperfect lawn doesn't bother us, we can let go of our concern and let the crabgrass grow.

Today, I will hold on only to my goals and expectations.
I will let go of those which give me no joy.

No great thing is created suddenly.
— EPICTETUS

It took many thousands of years for the Seven Wonders of the World to form, and they are truly awe-inspiring. We, too, can create great things, but we must be patient as the results of our efforts slowly evolve.

We can participate in the creation of a strong family as one of our great wonders, for a loving, close, caring family extends beyond the present generation. The love and family traditions we help create will be handed down from generation to generation. It's not so important that we see at once the greatness of what we do. What does matter is that we are able to make an effort and know that the reward will take time.

I can patiently work toward the creation
of new ideas and traditions, knowing that
rewards will be apparent in time.

∼ SEPTEMBER 8 ∼

Every great mistake has a halfway moment,
a split second when it can be recalled
and perhaps remedied.
—PEARL S. BUCK

We've all made decisions we've regretted. Regret doesn't change things, but we can learn to make better decisions in the future. Often there are moments in our decision-making process—especially in relationships—when we can still change our minds. At those times, we can reconsider what we want to say or do. Is it important enough to jeopardize a friendship? Sometimes it is, and that can't be helped.

But usually we discover we do want to preserve the relationship. We owe it to ourselves and our friends to look again, to think again, about what is being discussed or argued or decided. Sometimes, winning or being right isn't as important as the relationship.

I will take time to decide
what is important and what isn't.

SEPTEMBER 9

God, grant me the serenity to
accept the things I cannot change,
the courage to change the things I can,
and the wisdom to know the difference.
—THE SERENITY PRAYER

The Serenity Prayer has comforted millions of people who strive to cope with change, disappointments, chemical dependency, and all sorts of other problems. This prayer can comfort us as we deal with the realities of chronic illness.

When we're overcome with pain or disappointed about slow or little progress, this prayer can help us put our lives into focus. It helps us see if we're wasting time and energy on things we can't change, such as the chronic conditions we live with, how others feel, and the past. And just as important, this prayer points us toward the things that we can control—our attitude, our willingness to change, and the outcome of this day.

I pray for the wisdom to recognize the difference
between things I can and cannot change.

The real world is not easy to live in.
It is rough; it is slippery.
—CLARENCE DAY

What if the doctor has warned that the extra one hundred pounds is really going to cause death—imminently? What if the teenager who has been threatening to commit suicide succeeds? Does it take a crisis to shock us into action?

Too often we wait for an emergency situation to change our patterns of behavior. We can't change everything, but we do have it in our power to take back that which is in our control—our behavior.

We can take responsibility for our health, for our personal growth, and for our spiritual lives. We do not need to wait for an emergency.

Rather than waiting for a crisis to spur me into change,
I can take positive action on my own.

⮩ SEPTEMBER 11 ⮪

The world improves people according to
the dispositions they bring into it.
—Renier Giustina Michiel

Remember the phrase "Suck a sour lemon"? We have all known people who always look as though the world has handed them a bushel of lemons. No matter what the situation, no matter how happy other people would feel, these sour folks always have a reason to grimace.

Then there are the opposite kind—the ones who are dripping with sugar all the time. It doesn't matter how difficult their situation is, they always find reasons to smile. Both types are highly irritating and unrealistic, for life isn't always sweet and it's not always sour.

We can combine the two personality traits into a caring, compassionate human being who understands the highs and lows of life and who acts appropriately.

I can enhance my personal feelings of well-being
by improving how I act toward others.

*There is no more certain sign of a narrow mind,
of stupidity, and of arrogance, than to stand aloof
from those who think differently from us.*
— WALTER SAVAGE LANDOR

We all carry some opinions and beliefs formed long ago, with no thought as to how they continue to affect us. We may be closed to beliefs or ideas that differ from ours. Because of this we might be intolerant of other people, especially those who seem different from us.

Our beliefs and actions toward other people may come from fear—a fear of the unexpected, of the unknown, or of being wrong. We may resist examining the rules and beliefs governing our lives because we're not totally sure of them. Opening ourselves to new ideas is easier if we remind ourselves that we don't have to accept the ideas, just the people.

*I can fearlessly open myself to new ideas
and new people.*

*What next? Why ask? Next will come a demand
about which you already know all you need to know:
that its sole measure is your own strength.*
—DAG HAMMARSKJÖLD

Life is full of demands; we know and expect that. Most of us wish we knew about them ahead of time, but it's just not possible to prepare for stress. Negative stressors like a flat tire or a severe illness and positive stressors like a family reunion are typical of the demands placed on us throughout our lives.

Somehow, when these things happen, we manage to rise to the occasion. We may need to use all our resources—physical and spiritual—to cope, but we usually find within ourselves the strength and enthusiasm for the demands we face.

*By knowing that I will be able to
handle life's crises with deep inner strength,
I need not ask myself "What's next?" anymore.*

⸺ SEPTEMBER 14 ⸺

I loafe and invite my soul,
I lean and loafe at my ease
observing a spear of summer grass.
— WALT WHITMAN

Sometimes we may have wished we could be like Aladdin and have three wishes. We might have even made mental lists of the things we could ask for.

We know that just having material possessions is not a guarantee for happiness. We know there has to be a purpose to life beyond wealth, a reason to get out of bed each morning. Whatever our walk of life, whatever our state of health, we all need to feel worthwhile.

We can't rub magic lanterns, but we can create important reasons for living, such as a paid job, volunteer work, gardening or another hobby, or just plain relaxing. Idleness is sometimes good for improving our attitude.

The power of relaxation is a strong reason
to keep me from becoming stressed.

A fanatic is one who can't change his mind
and won't change the subject.
— WINSTON CHURCHILL

Nearly everyone who has ever undergone a time of high stress has an intense need to talk about it. A person who has lost someone close may talk almost constantly about it. People who are admitting that they must deal with chronic pain often feel the same need.

We can and should expect our friends to allow us the comfort of talking about our feelings and experiences. As people who are suffering from pain and who are often driven to recount an illness's history, we need to realize there is a point at which people no longer want to listen—they may want to leave instead. We must work—harder than we ever have before—to build a well-balanced life that has some happy or humorous stories to share.

I will leave room in my conversations for stories
that make me and my friends feel good.

*Made weak by time and fate, but strong in will
to strive, to seek, to find and not to yield.*
—ALFRED, LORD TENNYSON

Some privacy is given up when we develop a chronic illness, for doctors and nurses need to know details of our medical histories. We can develop new strengths to offset this loss—pride that we are taking care of ourselves and knowledge about our medical conditions.

Many of the private battles we fight concern our feelings about having a chronic health problem. We may have to yield on some points—privacy, dependence, time, and energy—but we can continue to make personal gains in spite of our health.

*Just because my health has changed does not mean
I need to yield on points that matter to my well-being.*

*Fight one more round. When your feet are
so tired you have to shuffle back to the center
of the ring, fight one more round.*
—JAMES J. CORBETT

One of the problems we most frequently hear about
when a person is ill, whether it be mentally or physically, is exhaustion. We tell our doctors, our friends,
anyone who will lend a willing ear, "I'm just so very
tired."

To live in the fullest sense of the word, we have to,
first of all, take care of ourselves. If what we feel is
physical exhaustion, then we must allow ourselves the
needed rest. We don't have to take on additional projects or commitments to prove ourselves. If, however,
our tiredness has an emotional base, we may have to
push ourselves—for just one more hour, for just one
more day—trusting that the energy will come.

*I will take care of myself this day.
I am getting stronger, emotionally and spiritually.*

∽ SEPTEMBER 18 ∽

*Our souls are hungry for meaning, for the sense that
we have figured out how to live so that our lives matter,
so that the world [will] be at least a little bit
different for our having passed through.*
— HAROLD KUSHNER

Even when we are no longer well, many of us continue
to hunger for learning. We reach out to connect with
other people and with book learning.

We continue to search on a deeper level as well. Not
surprisingly, spirituality often takes a backseat, for a
while, to the rigors of getting used to a changed medical
condition. Ultimately, our souls cry out for growth just
as our minds do, and we turn to our Higher Power for
comfort and understanding.

*My diminished health does not affect my drive for
meaning and for learning. I want and need to learn.*

Of a truth, men are mystically united:
a mystic bond of brotherhood makes all men one.
—THOMAS CARLYLE

At our parents' knees we listened, enraptured, as we heard tales of how life used to be. We could hardly believe that they had lived sooooo long. As we moved into our teens, perhaps our parents became pathetically inept in our eyes, not to regain their intelligence until we were older.

Now we see that our folks were able to learn from their mistakes and move forward—just as we move forward now. We have learned "what goes around comes around," and history repeats itself. Our parents imparted their greatest knowledge to us and lovingly shared with us their mistakes so we could benefit.

I will listen with respect to the ones I love.
I learn from them.

⌒ SEPTEMBER 20 ⌒

The natural wish of every human being,
the weakest as well as the wisest, seems to be,
to leave some memorial of themselves to posterity.
—Susan Edmonstone Ferrier

Each of us wants to leave evidence of our having lived.
To perpetuate our names, we may work and play hard
all our lives, or we may attempt to fine-tune sports skills
or handcrafts.

We become gradually aware that material records of
our lives will merely note our names and dates; they
will not record who we are and what we value. The
essence of each of us is found in each day, each moment. It is in living each day fully that we proclaim our
worth and reflect it to our loved ones. What really matters, we realize, is how we spend our present, not how
we try to manipulate the future. Living richly today is
our memorial.

I will use today as a complete gift unto itself,
not as a small brick for a future monument.

～ SEPTEMBER 21 ～

. . . Summer coming to an end. So we all try to keep it awake and stretch it out by squeezing in all the boating, picnicking, swimming. Sun, I crave all year.
—SISTER MARY KRAEMER

As the days begin to shorten and become cooler, we may suddenly be struck by the realization that the summer is over. With that thought might come the need to fill the last warm days with the many activities we postponed or, perhaps, forgot. At times like these, we may sense the need to hang on a little longer to the summer.

We do the same thing in other areas of our lives. At the moment we realize we are about to lose something very precious, that is when we value it most. Just before a dear friend moves away, we try to fill our days with togetherness. Knowing this can help us use our time more wisely and remind us to see the value in everyone and everything around us.

I will let others know I value them, and why.

*It is only the strong who are strengthened by suffering;
the weak are made weaker.*
— LION FEUCHTWANGER

In emergency health situations, people expect us to be a little more dependent and needy. But overly dependent behavior is not okay. We know it's not easy, when we are really suffering, to move to a position of strength, to create a new, mature attitude upon which we can base our behavior. It's difficult to unlearn old ways and to regroup our thoughts and actions. But using a "sickie" role is one of the behaviors we need to avoid.

Ultimately, no one is responsible for our mental and physical well-being but ourselves. As time goes by, we understand that we gain strength from our illnesses when we accept that responsibility.

*My health difficulties can strengthen
my attitude and my actions.*

⌒ SEPTEMBER 23 ⌒

*Physical courage, which despises all danger,
will make a man brave in one way; and moral courage,
which despises all opinion, will make a man brave in
another. The former would seem most necessary for
the camp; the latter for the council; but to constitute
a great man, both are necessary.*
—C. C. COLTON

We are blessed to have many kinds of courage. We just never expected to have them all tested during a course of several years! Our physical courage increases every time we face a new situation or a different medical problem. Although we're not grateful for the illness itself, it has provided the challenges that have prompted greater courage in us. We've also had to look more closely at our values and had to become stronger in protecting them. We're more conscious of the choices we make and how we make them, and we're grateful for that awareness.

I will continue to make healthy, moral choices.

⁓ SEPTEMBER 24 ⁓

To be what we are, and to become what we are
capable of becoming is the only end of life.
—ROBERT LOUIS STEVENSON

Mountain climbers, river rafters, and marathon racers all face the "challenge of a lifetime." We have heard that phrase before but may not have realized that our challenge of a lifetime would take a different form.

We all face challenges as we move through adulthood. In some instances—pain or illness, for example—we must face the obstacles placed in our way. We cannot choose to ignore or avoid them. One of our biggest challenges is the struggle to maintain a positive mental attitude. This is easier said than done when altered health patterns change lifestyles, but we can be on guard to think about "wellness" before "illness" and to remember we have been facing challenges all along.

I face challenges every day— some public,
but many private. I will try to do my personal best.

∼ SEPTEMBER 25 ∼

Fate chooses our relatives. We choose our friends.
— JACQUES BOSSUET

We had no choice—and still have no choice—as to whether our families are supportive and caring. Those of us who lived in negative or unnurturing families may find that we slip into similar situations as adults. Without realizing it, we may have fostered friendships that allow us to use the same old scripts—the same unhealthy scripts.

One of the things we've learned from our illnesses is that we must be willing to nurture ourselves. We need approval and love, and we have it within our power to give that gift to ourselves. We also can enter only into friendships based on these qualities, allowing us to be cared for and to care for others.

I choose today to work toward healthy,
loving friendships.

The modern sympathy with invalids is morbid.
Illness of any kind is hardly a thing
to be encouraged in others.
— OSCAR WILDE

When chronic illness strikes, there are no rules of social behavior we can fall back on. Nothing prepares us for the harsh reality of illness. There is a very delicate balance here. We want those who love us to understand, and we want them to help, but not to pity us.

We need to face squarely the changes that chronic illness brings, both for our loved ones and for us. By openly talking to each other about our problems of adjustment and loss, we can become less preoccupied with our losses and think more about the future. We will be less concerned with being "in-valid." We can move forth to a meaningful and valid life.

Facing the changes caused by chronic illness can,
in the long run, serve to make me stronger.

～ SEPTEMBER 27 ～

*We love persons . . . by reason of their defects
as well as of their qualities.*
—Jacques Maritain

There is a freedom in loving and being loved. The love
we have for other special people frees us to concentrate
on them, and we forget ourselves and our problems.
Often, these people—our friends and family members—
are loved by us not because we find perfection in them,
but because we magically seem to blend together, and
their faults become unimportant.

In being loved, we discover the same freedom. We
don't have to conceal our defects. We can be open. Certainly, we continue to work to free ourselves of defects,
but we do it for ourselves; we don't have to be perfect to
deserve love. Nonjudgmental love is one of the things
that frees us to make choices without fear.

*I treasure all the loving friendships I have.
They allow me to choose new directions
by accepting me where I am.*

*A positive, responsible person does not forget the past
harm which may have been done because of earlier
ignorance, thoughtlessness, or emotional limitations.*
— LEWIS F. PRESNALL

We've learned to forgive those who we felt have done harm to us. Our pain diminished over time, and we were able to let go of our bad feelings.

We are much less accepting of our own errors. Years later we may continue to mercilessly judge ourselves for past mistakes. We can forgive ourselves by offering ourselves the same understanding we have offered those we love. As we move to a new, gentler way of looking at ourselves, we can accept the mistakes we've made in the past and even understand them in context of where we were at the time.

*I can remember past mistakes I have made, but I will
be gentle with myself when I see how far I have come.*

Though we travel the world over to find the beautiful,
we must carry it with us or we find it not.
— RALPH WALDO EMERSON

Our culture encourages a quest for outer beauty, even
though we know it is more important to have inner
beauty. This is the beauty truly valued by others. We can
live joyfully; we can delight in discovering and enjoying
beauty. We are surrounded with loveliness in nature and
in people's thoughts, words, and deeds. To accept that
beauty, we must carry within ourselves a sensitivity, an
appreciation for what is offered, and that sensitivity is
a large part of the beauty we carry within us.

Life is full of beauty. I will keep my eyes open to the
beauty that is in others, in nature, and in myself.

⌒ SEPTEMBER 30 ⌒

There is no failure except in no longer trying.
—ELBERT HUBBARD

It would be tragic to live our lives without direction, to never try to fulfill any dreams. Perhaps we have felt that we do not have direction in our lives any longer or that we can't fulfill the lifelong dreams we had. By setting new goals and priorities in terms of today's reality, we can still have dreams and see them come true.

We might be tempted to resign ourselves to being failures, to set ourselves no new challenges, and to think of ourselves as victims. If we don't become fatigued with thoughts of resignation and failure, we will have the necessary energy to pursue new goals.

I am setting new goals that are realistic,
and I will invest my energy in them.

⌒ OCTOBER 1 ⌒

Solitude is not measured by the miles of space that intervene between a man and his fellows.
— HENRY DAVID THOREAU

Solitude is the time we choose to be alone, but it becomes loneliness when we believe we have no choice. When we are lonely, we feel trapped in a web of isolation.

Lonely people are caught in a trap with only themselves for company. There can be a difference between loneliness and aloneness—or solitude.

We are finding ways to create solitude from loneliness. We strive to fill our lives with meaningful experiences such as work, family, hobbies, and relationships with friends. As we enrich our lives with these activities, our alone time becomes solitude—a peaceful time to withdraw from the world and into thoughts, prayers, and meditation.

A moment of solitude today can enrich and replenish me.

～ OCTOBER 2 ～

*God wrote His loveliest
poem on the day
He made the first tall, poplar tree,
And set it high upon a pale-gold hill
For all the now enchanted earth to see.*
— GRACE NOLL

Autumn was such a wonderful time when we were youngsters. Raking meant gleefully jumping into mountains of leaves and later gathering with our families to watch the blazing piles.

We can still enjoy the trees and leaves around us. If we take time to observe even a single leaf, we will again be surprised at its beauty, its perfection. The golden or red or brown leaf is a small part of nature's balance.

We enjoyed trees before; we can find multiple ways to enjoy them now. Like all of the world around us, the leaves lend color, beauty, and meaning to our lives, if we only look.

*All natural beauty deserves
a second look before I turn away.*

Most of all, we seek to help them rise to what for most is the supreme challenge of their lives, by developing and enjoying their unique personalities to the fullest.
—BERNIE S. SIEGEL

Just living life, not enjoying it, is a tread-water posture some of us adopt in our lives. Afraid to get "too involved" in living, we wait for the worst to occur. We look for a guide, a leader, to direct our path to physical and spiritual survival.

At first, we may be devastated when we realize that no one else can direct us, guide us, or lead us out of the maze of emotions that accompanies a chronic illness. Others can help, but only if we lead. Gradually we're finding a unique strength within us, one we'd not known before, that enables us to direct our physical and spiritual programs with greater confidence.

I am on a continuing journey to accept the challenges of my life. Allowing my unique personality to surface is the beginning.

⟿ OCTOBER 4 ⟿

The bitter and the sweet come from the outside,
the hard from within, from one's own efforts.
—ALBERT EINSTEIN

Too often we expect to have lives in which only happy events occur and no one is ever hurt. Instead of tears and sadness, we expect only happiness. In doing this, we do not face life realistically. By ignoring all the problems around us—our own and others' as well—we skim the surface of life.

When we face reality, we begin our real journey. A life well lived is not one of constant happiness and joy. More often, it is the life as lived by someone who has known intense pain and extreme disappointment. Our negative experiences give us that opportunity to be strengthened within.

All my experiences give me a chance to grow.

⚘ OCTOBER 5 ⚘

Be patient with everyone, but above all with yourself.
—St. Francis de Sales

Like fine cheese, we wait, as we grow older, to ripen properly. We would like to hurry the process along, but haste won't serve us well in the long run. We have learned to let others take their time to mature and to become responsible adults, but often when it comes to ourselves, we are quick to anger at our own mistakes. We frequently are not as forgiving of ourselves as we are of others.

Maturity arrives when we understand that some of the goals we thought were crucial are really unattainable and that it really doesn't matter. Maturity is a frame of mind where we learn to be pleased with what we can accomplish. We can find contentment in just living our days as best we can.

I recognize there is no magic moment
when I will become a fully mature adult.
Maturity is an attitude that conveys peace with myself.

Every human being is a problem in search of a solution.
—ASHLEY MONTAGU

Despite the occasional distance or coolness that many of us sense within, we are also aware of wellsprings of emotion, ready to flow with feelings that have been long hidden. It sometimes takes a crisis, such as illness, chemical dependency, or loss of a loved one to literally drive us to seek help.

Trying to uncover deeply hidden painful emotions can feel like a treacherous path to follow, and some of us may be tempted to stop trying. But if we honestly open ourselves to these feelings, we can begin to know ourselves better and to build healthier and more mature relationships.

Change can be frightening, especially when I've been hiding from my own emotions. If there is a problem, dealing with my emotions is part of the solution.

Honor your challenges, for those spaces that you label
as dark are actually there to bring you more light.
— SANAYA ROMAN

Many of us have wondered whether we should begin using adaptive-living aids openly. We worry about what people would think if they saw us using equipment that brands us as handicapped. We fear embarrassment. Some folks never solve the problem, and they stay home, trapped by their fears of being noticed, of being different. It's difficult to forfeit the anonymity of being the same as everyone else.

One thing is certain—without special gadgets, we have to ask for help. So, with foresight and a fierce sense of independence, many of us grasp any opportunity to "do" for ourselves. We can use aids because they will assist and support our zest for life.

I will risk being different. By using adaptive devices
I can remain more independent.

～ OCTOBER 8 ～

Love is all we have,
the only way that each can help the other.
—EURIPIDES

We may tend to love our family members only with qualifications. Only if they don't complain about their problems. Only if they are more successful. Perhaps we don't say this directly, but we might be communicating these qualifications to our loved ones by holding back or by making indirect suggestions as to how they should live their lives.

We may be able to give our love more fully if we remember how much we need acceptance. We don't want to receive love that is prefaced by "only if . . ." Only if we don't complain. Only if we stop talking about our illnesses. We all need the comfort and support of love based on what we are, not on what others think we can or should be. Our loved ones need the same thing.

Knowing I am loved and can love others
in an unqualified manner strengthens me.

⌒ OCTOBER 9 ⌒

*Bitterness and anger seem to be very closely related
and are interchangeable words for the same emotion.*
—Robert Lovering

Bitterness and anger don't arrive out of the blue when there is a health change. Chronic illness doesn't cause these reactions, but it may bring these and other feelings to light.

If negative emotions and attitudes cause us pain or embarrassment, if we are unhappy with ourselves, it may be time to take a personal inventory. How do we act toward other people? What do we expect? Do we create our own problems?

We can change negatives into positives, but it requires time and great emotional effort. Our attitudes do improve when we want to change, when we're willing to grow, and when we're patient with ourselves.

*I can begin today to change my negative emotions
by admitting them and asking for the help I need.*

⚬ OCTOBER 10 ⚬

But if a man happens to find himself . . .
he has a mansion which he can inhabit
with dignity all the days of his life.
—James Michener

"If only," we think, "I could regain that joy, that feeling of being so pleased with myself that I had as a child." If we think about it, we might decide that the child didn't disappear; it may still be waiting to be freed once again.

We can pause and look at what we have become as adults. If we seek self-worth by pleasing or impressing others, we may have stopped listening to that childlike voice that tells us to trust ourselves. Dignity, self-worth, contentment—these things grow out of a sense of self, not from the opinions of others.

The choices I make today will be
based on my own values.

～ OCTOBER 11 ～

Power said to the world, "You are mine."
The world kept it prisoner on her throne.
Love said to the world, "I am thine."
The world gave it the freedom of her house.
— RABINDRANATH TAGORE

We all need to test our spiritual muscles. At first those muscles may seem weak. It's natural after a lengthy bout with illness to wonder why we were chosen for pain, misery, or illness.

After a time, we become ready to learn more about our own spirituality. We open our minds and our hearts. As we explore this wonderful side of ourselves, we discover our worth, our strengths, our wholeness. And we discover that we are not alone, that a Higher Power is sharing His strength and peace with us.

Today, I will learn more about my spirituality
than I knew yesterday. I will feel the peace and
strength given to me by my Higher Power.

Joy . . . is found only in the good things of the soul.
— PHILO

Every day has its ups and downs—its good and bad moments. The joys that today offers must be personally claimed, by each of us, or they will pass by unnoticed.

The events that cause a joyful experience are different for all individuals. We sometimes share joyful experiences with other people. Watching an infant walk for the first time can be a shared joy and a lasting memory. Recognizing that our friends, or perhaps even ourselves, have found help in dealing with personal problems or harmful behaviors can also be joyful experiences.

Joy can also be a private time—fishing on a lovely morning, watching the petals of a flower unfold, or being part of a growing relationship. All contribute to our sense of well-being.

*In this day, I will be aware of
the people and activities that give me joy.*

～ OCTOBER 13 ～

You learn to build your roads on today,
because tomorrow's ground is too uncertain for plans,
and futures have a way of falling down in mid-flight.
—VERONICA SHOFFSTAL

We may have lived a significant portion of our adult lives planning for the future. Although we must make some provision for tomorrow—savings accounts, wills, pension plans—our attempts to live a full, rewarding life must be made each day.

Growth occurs in the present; it's never accomplished if it's postponed until tomorrow. Each day we choose the direction of our lives, whether we know it or not. Either we take positive steps toward better goals and stronger values, or we move not at all by "planning" our lives in some uncertain future.

I will make good choices for myself
in the reality of today.

⟶ OCTOBER 14 ⟵

Nothing sharpens sight like envy.
—THOMAS FULLER

It's natural to want to own things—a house, a car, nice clothes, a boat. Once in a while we are able to save and buy some things we like, but more often we have to set priorities and choose which items really matter to us most.

Almost all of us know someone who *does* seem to have it all—materially—and we may be envious. Perhaps, at those times we can better serve our needs if we reexamine our values and cast our eyes toward other people who have the things we really want—peace of mind, a loving nature, spiritual depth, and an unjealous nature. Those "things" may be what we should strive to own. These qualities can be purchased only with time and enrich our lives more than mere material objects ever could.

I will take inventory of my qualities,
not my possessions.

⌒ OCTOBER 15 ⌒

We cannot tear out a single page from our life,
but we can throw the whole book into the fire.
— GEORGE SAND

During those darkest times, we may not be able to think beyond this moment, this pain, this loss. All we're aware of is this tiny piece of time, and it casts its darkness on all we remember and all we see in the future.

This moment is a fraction of a lifetime; this feeling is just one perception among thousands we've experienced. We owe it to ourselves to be sure of what we are experiencing before discarding the entire book in order to rid ourselves of one hated page. If needed, we can explore our emotions with a professional. We can work within a group of people who understand. We can wait a while to see what our lives will hold. We can look for change outside and inside ourselves.

My feelings are real, but so is the chance that
better things lie ahead. I pray for patience.

⟿ OCTOBER 16 ⟿

Don't let life discourage you;
everyone who got where he is had to begin where he was.
— RICHARD L. EVANS

There's an old adage that good teachers still use: Start the child from where he is. In fact, we all have to begin from where we are. We may, at first, have a tendency to measure all our successes with our healthy life before our medical condition changed. Changed circumstances can play havoc with our lives.

Now, we may have to set more realistic goals in order to reach them. We can still begin new jobs or new relationships. We begin over and over again throughout a lifetime—with or without a long-term medical situation. What matters most is how successfully we can handle the change. We'll do fine as long as we remember we have started anew many times—successfully.

I will not be discouraged by changes in my life.
I have coped before, and I will again.

~ OCTOBER 17 ~

Maturity: among other things —
not to hide one's strength out of fear
and consequently live below one's best.
— DAG HAMMARSKJÖLD

The fear of being different is a powerful force in our lives, especially in the early times after a chronic illness is diagnosed. We fear being recognized as a victim of an illness, and we become afraid of any recognition at all.

We don't want to live with this unreasonable fear, and we begin to understand that healthy thinking requires us to develop and use our many strengths. We stop denying and start accepting. The voice of our individuality begins to speak, loudly and clearly, and we answer with definitive action. We start to face our problems, to accept the ways in which we differ from others, and to rejoice in our strengths.

I won't hide my strengths,
for they are the means to life at its best.

～ OCTOBER 18 ～

He that can't endure the bad,
will not live to see the good.
—YIDDISH PROVERB

Maturity means taking the bitter with the sweet. Wisdom is the realization that sometimes the two are interrelated. An example of this is chronic illness. At first, we might have been bitter because the quality of our lives was changed.

Now, with a clearer perspective and greater maturity, we realize that many of the sweeter aspects of our lives today have grown out of our learning to cope with chronic illness. We live more in the moment, rather than always pursuing some distant goal. Our values reflect a stronger sense of self; they emphasize people over things. For many of us, the growth, the joy, and the self-esteem that now sweeten our lives come from the bitter experiences of chronic illness.

I accept that my life experiences will be both
good and bad. Although my illness is unwanted,
I have been strengthened by it.

~ OCTOBER 19 ~

There must be something strangely sacred in salt.
It is in our tears and in the sea.
— KAHLIL GIBRAN

Emotion plays around a person's face, making it strained or relaxed. We say we can "read" someone else's face. Few of us burst into spontaneous tears or laughter, but instead first show slight emotion on our faces or in the way we speak.

Laughter is instrumental to our well-being, but tears are also essential to our emotional survival. When we finally release the emotions we feel and the dams break loose, the tears are healing. They allow us to cleanse ourselves of pent-up angers, fears, and frustrations.

I know crying is a human characteristic.
I will not be ashamed of my need to cry,
for tears are part of my human experience.

*By a tranquil mind I mean nothing else
than a mind well ordered.*
— MARCUS AURELIUS ANTONINUS

When we are diagnosed as having a permanent medical condition, we may think we'll never know tranquility again. Before too long, though, we realize that whether we are entirely healthy or not, we bring to our new challenge the same value system we always had. We can still find peace and serenity in our lives, for we continue to live our lives as well as we are able.

We owe it to ourselves to search out tranquility—a state in which we feel extremely peaceful, at ease with our inner strength, with nature, and with our sense of higher purpose. Walking hand in hand with tranquility creates harmony, a time when our thoughts are orderly and we feel little distress.

*I will work on keeping a peaceful mind
in order to smooth out my rougher days.*

Business runs after nobody;
people cling to it of their own free will
and think that to be busy is a proof of happiness.
—LUCIUS ANNAEUS SENECA

Sometimes we need to keep busy just to fill time. After a loss or health change, we may have great amounts of time to fill. We may turn to busywork—work having no significance but marking time as we move toward yet another adjustment. Tool-shop organizing, closet cleaning, and other tasks might be ploys we need, emotionally, to perform in rote fashion.

When we are adjusting, we may need to be busy—to think, to decide on new plans of action, and to move forward. We won't need busywork, and we'll be able to make gains again. As we make our adjustments, very, very slowly, the purpose of our lives will return.

I will put effort into my days to find meaning.
It may be difficult to stay busy, but I can do it.

This is the bitterest knowledge among men,
to have much knowledge but no power.
—HERODOTUS

We have the power to influence others' lives only when we share what we have learned. If we fail to or refuse to recognize the value of our knowledge, we force ourselves into a sort of isolation and—worse still—deprive others of our insights.

We know how to handle intricate personal relationships and delicate problems. We have gained the emotional stability to allow ourselves to depend on others and on our Higher Power. We can share this knowledge with others, not to serve our own needs, but to help our fellow human beings.

A loving power is mine when I gently share
the knowledge I have with others.

The more passionately we love life,
the more intensely we experience the joy of life.
—JURGEN MOLTMAN

While we would occasionally like to hide from the real-life drama around us, we know it's not a healthy way to live. Instead we live the drama, love it, cry with it, and at times even hate it.

Choosing to live life on its terms brings enthusiasm and passion into our experiences. Our decision to love life—despite the highs and lows—allows us to delight in the highs and to accept the lows as unavoidable, but momentary, setbacks. Although hiding from reality can sometimes insulate us from pain, it also blinds us to the joys and wonderment of living fully.

I choose to be enthusiastic about my life.

～ OCTOBER 24 ～

*We conceal it from ourselves in vain —
we must always love something.*
—BLAISE PASCAL

Not knowing how to love may imperil our very existence. Although love doesn't literally nourish our bodies, not being able to love strips us of our humanness.

Romantic love is only one part of our capacity to love, for there is also the ability to love our friends, our families, and our fellow human beings. The ripple effect of our well-being will spread, both within us and from us, and we will begin to nourish our souls as well.

We also learn to love ourselves—all that we are. Self-love enhances our self-image. A strong sense of esteem enhances our entire lives.

I need to love and be loved. It is essential to my psychic well-being that I understand the importance of loving.

The more things you love,
the more you are interested in, the more you enjoy,
the more you have left when anything happens.
—ETHEL BARRYMORE

Now is a good time for us to pursue our interests and to nurture both new and old relationships. We understand so well how easily and quickly our circumstances can change. This understanding nudges us to expand our experiences.

No one of us is immune from the troubles of life. Whether the problem is loss of a job or loss of a home, good health, or a dear friend, we all suffer at one time or another. Keeping our lives as full as possible with the love of good people and the challenge of activities provides support even when times get tough.

Tragedies and hard times will affect me,
but I know I have the ability to move on.

～ OCTOBER 26 ～

*Don't part with your illusions. When they are gone,
you may still exist, but you have ceased to live.*
— MARK TWAIN

Even as we approached young adulthood, we clung to
our dreams about the future. In those days it may have
seemed to us that anything was possible.

It's not immature to hold on to a dream, even when
we know the dream is unlikely to come true. Bald men
wish for a full head of hair. Some of us wish we still had
young skin. Even though a long-term medical condition
has become part of our lives, many of us still hold on to
the illusions of our health being restored.

Now we have a few more years—or decades—behind
us. We accept that some things are possible and some
are not. Most of us are comfortable with that knowledge. And still we hope.

*I hold dearly to many of my illusions. The possibilities
of what might occur keep my days full of excitement.*

Better be alone than in bad company.
— THOMAS FULLER

Most of us have had the experience of being befriended by someone who seems to want to spend every waking moment in our company. At first, we may be delighted with the attention and enjoy the excitement of the developing relationship. Then, suddenly we feel smothered. The other person gives us no time alone; he or she is such a constant presence that we feel out of touch with ourselves.

We seem to have to choose between crushing our new friend or submitting to the constant intrusion, but first we may need to remind ourselves that we have the right to create the framework of our days. If bad company or just constant company is not our choice, we are free to say, "I need more time alone." This isn't a rejection of others; it's an affirmation of ourselves and our need for solitude.

I can find a healthy balance between
my time with others and my time alone.

~ OCTOBER 28 ~

Yesterday is not ours to recover,
but tomorrow is ours to win or lose.
—LYNDON B. JOHNSON

We can cherish our yesterdays or even regret them, but we can never live them again. The past is behind us; the future lies ahead. We may sometimes be saddened by the thought that the future might be shorter than our past, but we find comfort in remembering that the future is real and promising; the past is neither.

To find only positives in the past and negatives in the future robs us of one of our greatest gifts—time—and time is what the past can't give us. Yesterday's gifts to us are memories, and an occasional backward glance to what once was is natural. But we grow mentally and spiritually by living in this day and planning for tomorrow.

I accept the gifts of yesterday's memories,
today's reality, and tomorrow's dreams.

∽ OCTOBER 29 ∽

You may talk on all subjects save one,
namely, your maladies.
— RALPH WALDO EMERSON

Casual conversations have an unspoken rule: never, never tell about our pain, our misery, our difficulties. Ironically, the stars of social gatherings are often the ones who have just suffered an accident or injury. We show interest and concern for new and obvious problems; we often ignore ongoing ones. A leg cast has glamor; a wheelchair has none.

We can understand this. Human nature finds adventure in broken bones or neck braces. It also finds reassurance because these injuries are temporary and the victim will be as good as new in a matter of weeks. Many people can't identify with the permanence of chronic illness, but we can educate them about our social concerns without provoking pity.

My life becomes more balanced when I enjoy
social activities as social— not medical— events.

⟶ OCTOBER 30 ⟵

*We can have a hand in
our own daily miracle of health.*
—LEWIS F. PRESNALL

Some things we cannot change or control, and one of those most certainly is the limiting nature of illnesses. But we're not alone. We have surely learned by now that all people have to deal with handicaps or limitations—physical, psychological, or emotional. Like all other people, we are challenged to live a fulfilling life within the limitations placed upon us.

What matters most is that even though we may have a long-term health problem, we can learn to dwell on wellness, not on illness. Limitations certainly affect how we live our lives, but they need not alter the quality of who we are. It's up to us to choose whether we will be all we are intended to be.

*There are large areas which I can still control in my life,
and that gives me hope.*

The human body is the best picture of the human soul.
— LUDWIG WITTGENSTEIN

As people walk down the street, we can usually spot those with a sense of pride in themselves. How people look is often an indicator of their self-esteem. The changes in our lives challenge us to continue feeling good about ourselves despite stress or diminished health. Any change can be frightening. Unfortunately, sometimes we let problems overtake us, and we begin to look and act like people who feel unwell.

We can take stock of our lives at this time and remember how much we can still do well. We are capable individuals; we can make our own decisions about how we want to conduct our lives. This renewed awareness strengthens our self-esteem, and the image we convey to others is one of pride.

There are some things I just cannot change.
Today, I will dwell on what I can do for myself.

Old age, to the unlearned, is winter;
to the learned, it is harvest time.
— JUDAH LEIB LAZEROV

Too many of us fear old age, for it is seen all too often as merely the bridge between retirement and senility or death. This, of course, is only a myth. Advancing years do not automatically mean poor health or dependency.

We should always be aware of the pride and integrity that come with old age. Some older people stand as role models to youth. Decades of work have honed skills that can and should continue to be used in various ways. There is always more to learn and more to do. We can use our time to pursue interests and to develop any skills that give us joy.

I will not be frightened of growing older,
for I intend to do so with the pride and integrity
developed with age and experience.

*Grace is the absence of everything that indicates
pain or difficulty, hesitation or incongruity.*
—WILLIAM HAZLITT

Grace is the power to look within ourselves and become
stronger. When we're truly gracious, we try to put ourselves in another's place so we can imagine how that
person might feel. This becomes an especially important issue when we are physically impaired, for those
around us will take their cue from our behavior.

Trying to cope with the internal forces of health
changes can be very lonely. When we need to use as-
sistive devices such as canes, walkers, or wheelchairs,
other people may at first not know quite how to react.
We can help ease their discomfort and guide their reactions by our positive actions.

*I will be gracious to others by being aware
of their level of comfort when we are together.*

*It is well to give when asked, but it is better to give
when unasked through understanding.*
—KAHLIL GIBRAN

Some of us wonder how we will live the rest of our lives
with the problems we are currently carrying. The days
loom long, with no specific goals in sight; so it is up to
us to formulate new plans and goals for ourselves.

These plans—social, spiritual, academic, or volunteer—are good for us if they revolve around other
people, many of whom have even greater problems
than ours. Sharing our hope, faith, and varied experiences with others who also suffer is a caring gesture and
an opportunity to see ourselves and our problems more
clearly within the total human picture.

*Today, I will choose some way to help myself and others.
Sharing my experiences and skills keeps me
in touch with my humanness.*

~ NOVEMBER 4 ~

You cannot create experience. You must undergo it.
—ALBERT CAMUS

Who among us hasn't wanted to play with or read to a pleading child? Who hasn't thought of volunteering some time so others—and we—could have happier and richer lives? We may have put off or refused these opportunities because we felt overwhelmed by the limitations of a chronic illness. Perhaps we felt like victims who had lost an essential power to control our lives.

Our days are increasingly better when we understand that all experience, good and bad, isn't orchestrated by us—and it never was. Yet this doesn't mean we are helpless. We now see choices and chances to let our actions be positive life-affirming statements. We see opportunities for sharing, for joining in, and for reaching out. And we take them.

I will concentrate on making good choices,
not just easy choices.

~ NOVEMBER 5 ~

I remember those happy days and often wish
I could speak into the ears of the dead the gratitude
which was due to them in life and so ill-returned.
—Gwyn Thomas

We respond to loss in predictable ways. One common response to loss—whether of a loved one or of good health—is regret. "I should have told him how much he was loved" or, "I wish I'd told her I was sorry for what I said." These statements of regret are much like the regrets accompanying chronic illness. "I wish I'd pursued my dreams when I was healthy." We move out of our sadness only when we are able to remember that our only mistake was a human one—always believing there would be more time to say and do the things we wanted. Our healing is complete when we bring this awareness to the present, when we say and do positive things today.

Letting go of past regrets frees me to
be a more loving person today.

∽ NOVEMBER 6 ∽

*To achieve great things we must live
as though we were never going to die.*
— VAUVENARQUES

Of all the limitations we face, one of the greatest is actually one we impose upon ourselves. We limit ourselves by believing that it's too late to go back to school, to change careers, or to start something new. We artificially restrict ourselves because we misunderstand the concept of time.

We can decide if time is a friend or an enemy. It's our enemy when we shy away from new experiences. But when we willingly take unsteady steps into unknown territory by lifting a brush to canvas or finally learning to drive a car or applying for the job we've always wanted, then time is our friend. We have all the time in the world because we have *this* moment, this day, and that is all the time we need to begin great things.

*I am the only one who can decide
which great things I will begin today.*

⌒ NOVEMBER 7 ⌒

Night brings our troubles to the light,
rather than banishes them.
—LUCIUS ANNAEUS SENECA

One of our greatest coping skills is setting realistic expectations. In doing so, we're less likely to moan and complain. We're not so filled with self-pity. We are learning to use all our resources when we lie awake struggling with physical or emotional pain.

We can help ourselves by making our bedroom surroundings as pleasant as possible. Adding small items, such as flowers, bookcases, and a mini–reading lamp isn't just a cosmetic improvement. It's admitting that we might be spending some wakeful time in there. Some nights might be sleepless, but admitting it and preparing for it may make the experience less frightening and more restful.

If I can't sleep,
I can relax in the comfort of my bedroom.

*We often experience more regret over the part we have
left, than pleasure over the part we have preferred.*
—JOSEPH ROUX

We may sometimes think about past loves, jobs we turned down, or educations we didn't pursue. This nostalgic inventory may give us more regret than joy.

A more accurate picture of our lives is found in the things we've chosen. We can start with the communities in which we live. Quickly, we find ourselves listing such intangibles as spiritual experiences, family times of togetherness, friendships, and love. Seeing life more clearly as a balance between mistakes and triumphs, disappointments and joys, can encourage us to expect the same balance each day.

*I have less regret for what I've lost
when I focus on the many good things I've chosen.*

⌣ NOVEMBER 9 ⌣

Faith is a living and unshakeable confidence,
a belief in the grace of God so assured that a man
would die a thousand deaths for its sake.
— MARTIN LUTHER

When a crisis occurs—a death in the family or perhaps a chronic illness—many of us pass through the "Why me?" phase. We may become confused and feel we have been personally selected for bad times. Our faith may be shaken. It can take us a while to recognize that we still have abiding faith in our Higher Power. Time passes and as life gains some semblance of normalcy again, we understand there are no easy answers, but our faith has carried us through a difficult time.

Eventually, our belief in a Power greater than ourselves takes hold, rather firmly, until we feel an even stronger sense of faith and purpose than before.

As I gain my own strengths, I am more able to extend
my beliefs to include my Higher Power once again.

～ NOVEMBER 10 ～

It is easier to confess a defect than to claim a quality.
—MAX BEERBOHM

It is easy to simply admit our character defects—and then do nothing about them. The difficult part is asking God—however we picture God—to remove our defects and then live with the choices we have made.

We may have apologized to friends, and then added, "but I've always been that way." Or, "I just can't seem to help it." We might have used such excuses to avoid looking honestly at ourselves. When we sincerely examine our character defects and have the desire to change, our confessions to others no longer are made with excuses. Instead, we admit our flaws, ask our Higher Power to remove them, and then take responsibility for working toward qualities we admire.

*My defects can be changed once I admit them
and begin to work on eliminating them.*

*Pray that your loneliness may spur you into finding
something to live for, great enough to die for.*
—DAG HAMMARSKJÖLD

The first time we go through a festive season without
our spouse or a dear friend or beloved child, we may
wonder if we can get through it. Pity overwhelms us as
we think, "Surely no one has felt as bad as I do right
now." Pain increases our loneliness, and we feel crushed
by the holiday preparations the rest of the world seems
to be making.

We can struggle out of this self-imposed misery by
using the strategies that have helped us cope with our
chronic illnesses. Patience tells us that this, too, shall
pass. Selflessness shows us others who need compassion more than we do. Spirituality reminds us that our
pain and sadness can be entrusted to the loving care of
our Higher Power.

*I know the holidays can be difficult,
and if I take them one day at a time, I will do just fine.*

~ NOVEMBER 12 ~

Life is the enjoyment of emotion,
derived from the past and aimed at the future.
—ALFRED, LORD WHITEHEAD

Life sails by much more quickly than we expect it to. When our children were young, it seemed as though endless years stretched ahead for us to nurture and teach them; suddenly they are in college or married with children of their own.

Each day must be lived to its fullest, for we shall never be able to recapture it again. The memories we create today can enrich the present and even future years. Making good memories serves us well.

It is our wish to fully enjoy life and, if we can't, to attempt to correct those problems that keep us from fully enjoying what we do have. Then we can once again look to a full and wonderful future.

I will work to deal with those facets of my life
which cause me pain.

Meditation is not a means to an end.
It is both the means and the end.
—KRISHNAMURTI

There is a current trend toward reading meditation books, which we're familiar with. We tend to use meditations as enlarged thoughts for the day. Some of us begin our days with a meditation; others of us use them as a final thought before bed.

Meditation encourages deep and comforting thoughts. How we meditate has little importance, for customs are different across the cultures. What does matter is that we are turning to rich spiritual resources, so that each day we can give some serious time to our most pertinent thoughts and to improving ourselves.

When I meditate, I have a special thought
to carry with me throughout the day.
I know I am doing something important for myself.

⁓ NOVEMBER 14 ⁓

Rest is not a matter of doing absolutely nothing.
Rest is repair.
—DANIEL W. JOSSELYN

Every once in a while the burdens of our lives get us down. We just can't be optimistic all the time. It's so important to know that we can let go of those burdens for a day or two; in fact, we owe it to ourselves.

Too many of us feel guilty if we succumb to our feelings of sadness, disgust, anger, or exhaustion. Why? Having a medical problem doesn't make us any more or less exempt from the problems that face everybody else. There will be days when there seems to be no reason to get out of bed. That's okay. We can take a mental health day by relaxing. We can pamper ourselves every once in a while to rejuvenate the physical and emotional strength needed to face our world.

I can simplify my life by giving myself
this day for relaxing.

NOVEMBER 15

*There is always room for improvement, you know —
it's the biggest room in the house.*
—LOUISE HEATH LEBER

Accepting criticism is very hard, even when it's given constructively. As small children, we may have bristled at suggestions about our drawings or toy houses we made. We liked things to be the way we wanted them to be.

Not everyone is so talented and sensitive that they can offer criticism without it hurting. We do ourselves justice when we learn to listen to most criticism. Of course, we retain the right to disagree.

We understand that criticism is often tempered with love and understanding. A receptiveness to criticism helps us become less rigid and more willing to change.

*I can accept criticism and try to change
when it will benefit me.*

The future is an opaque mirror.
Anyone who tries to look into it sees nothing but
the dim outlines of an old and worried face.
—JIM BISHOP

Perhaps we spend too much time looking into mirrors and being critical of what we see. There is no stage in life when we are wholly contented with what we see, but as we mature we gradually recognize that our lives are multidimensional. Now we know that there will be periods of time when we are more pensive, more introspective—and times when life will just roll along, with no concern from us.

Acceptance of our appearance gives us the time and energy to work on our inner self. We look to the future by trying to prepare, and we live in the present by understanding that what we look like is not as important as what we do.

Today, I will decide which changes can
give me and others the most joy.

The people plan, and God laughs.
— YIDDISH PROVERB

Through the ages our ancestors have recognized that sometimes what happens is due to a purely random selection. Natural disasters occur, accidents happen, and people are in the wrong places at the wrong times.

But what about being in the right place at the right time? It's not very often that we hear those stories. We hear about tragedies and real triumphs. What we don't hear are stories about people like us, who struggle along, doing the best they can, hoping for a break. We have learned there are times to let go of unrealistic plans and to let our Higher Power have a hand in our lives. By letting go we create our own well-being.

I make my plans and hope for success, knowing there is a Power greater than me who has the final word.

Life is not a static thing.
—EVERETT M. DIRKSON

Sometimes change occurs so slowly within us that we don't notice it. We accept it and may even welcome it when it happens gradually, but we're less likely to accept those changes that arrive suddenly. Abrupt change doesn't fit what we expect and can cause chaos in our lives.

When we finally realize we can't prevent changes from happening, but can only alter our reactions to these changes, they become easier to accept. We can't stop our declining health either, but we can certainly understand the influence a positive attitude can have on our lives.

I will accept the things I cannot change.

There is no formula for easy living.
Anyone who says he has one is either joking or lying.
—HAROLD RUSSELL

We all have, in our mind's eye, a picture of what life would be like if we were healthy and wealthy and could do whatever we wanted with our days. If given the choice between health and sickness, wealth and poverty, most people would choose the former of both. Yet, there are no assurances of easy living no matter how healthy or wealthy we are.

When our wish to "have it easy" becomes a pre-occupation—like living with severe pain—our whole system can become stressed. We need to recognize that this wish for having it easy creates stress that we could avoid. Ironically, to escape this stress, we need to return to the reality of our own beautiful lives.

I have no guarantee for easy living,
but I am guaranteed the chance to change
and grow as often as I want to.

～ NOVEMBER 20 ～

There is no hope unmingled with fear,
and no fear unmingled with hope.
—BARUCH SPINOZA

Most of us are frightened each time we go through a major life change, for we fear what we do not know. We thought we had our lives planned. Because a crisis occurs unexpectedly, there is no way to prepare for a burglary, a broken leg, or the loss of a loved one. These events can throw us and our lives into a tailspin.

If the event is short-lived, like a bad case of the flu or a minor injury, we forget it quickly. If, however, the effects are long-lasting, we work to incorporate them into our daily living. Adapting in this way forces us to look for the positive parts of the day. We get into the habit of remembering good times and we hope— even expect—better times will come.

I can see that positive action and thought is needed.
I will find good people and events in this day.

To most of us the real life is the life we do not lead.
　—OSCAR WILDE

We don't enjoy feeling envious, but there are times when we find ourselves wishing we had what others do. "I wish my body could do what hers does." "I wish I didn't have to take all this medicine. He doesn't have to."

After feeling envious, we need to return to our own lives with enthusiasm. While we may not be able to do what others do or have what others have, our lives are filled with experiences that can make us rich and able people. Regardless of who we are, what we own, or how we live, each of us is living a very important life—complete with pain, memories, and pleasure.

I respect myself and this life I am living.
Today, I will concentrate on its joys and treasures.

Just pray for a thick skin and a tender heart.
—RUTH GRAHAM

There are times when we become angry or hurt or disappointed by the words or actions of our friends. When we react in any of these ways, we are focusing on them instead of us. "He hurt my feelings," we might say, or, "She made me angry." These statements point out the error in our reasoning. No one can "make" us feel a certain way.

Our lives are happier and our emotions more even when we realize we are choosing our reactions. "I let myself be angry (or hurt or disappointed)." Knowing this gives us a choice in how we let others affect us. We can be less sensitive to real or imagined wrongs. Instead, we can use our sensitivity to understand the pain of others.

I will be more loving toward my friends by overlooking their flaws and underlining their strengths.

What's a man's first duty?
The answer is brief: To be himself.
—Henrik Ibsen

We may tend to neglect ourselves, not just physically, but emotionally and spiritually as well. We are generally aware of what we're doing when we don't eat right or get enough sleep, but we often are blind to our neglect of inner needs. Each of us needs privacy, to think, to plan, to be away from the everyday clamor of our lives.

We can take time for ourselves, even if it's just a brief moment now and then. So we can assess our lives. So we can relax, alone. So we can pray. So we can be ourselves.

I will not hide from myself under the guise of
being too busy. I can take time, just for myself,
to be aware of my personal needs.

~ NOVEMBER 24 ~

Kindness in words creates confidence.
Kindness in thinking creates profoundness.
Kindness in giving creates love.
—Lao Tzu

As the holiday season approaches, we watch young families being swept up with the joy of the holiday season. It's natural to feel some self-pity, for it seems as though no holiday will ever be the same as the ones gone by.

Now it's time to make new memories. We can create them for ourselves. Who but ourselves do we have to blame for not having a good time during the holidays? Envying other people and the joy they share will serve no one. Have we shared with anyone today? Aren't there people who can be touched by our kind thoughts or actions? Can't we give of ourselves unselfishly? The holiday season is not about isolation; it is about reaching out.

I have the ability to bring old and new
holiday traditions to others.

Be a football to Time and Chance,
the more kicks the better, so that you inspect the
whole game and know its utmost law.
— RALPH WALDO EMERSON

There's something attractive about living a controlled life, a life in which we're never embarrassed or disappointed or foolish. Perhaps it's safety we seek when we try to control everyone and everything around us. As is so often true, we can't get one thing without forfeiting another. In this case, if we choose safety, we lose spontaneity and excitement.

Although we don't want to take dangerous risks or make foolish choices when clearly better ones present themselves, we may want to loosen our tight, controlling grasp on our lives. To live fully and joyously, we do want and need to examine the range of experiences life offers. Yes, we may get a few bumps and bruises, but we'll also find joy and contentment.

Today, I will welcome the unexpected in my life.

Trees and fields tell me nothing;
men are my teachers.
— PLATO

Our earliest teachers were our parents, and from them, if we were lucky, we learned unqualified love and acceptance and developed our religious beliefs. Later, trained professionals taught us specific subject matter. We also learned ethics from our instructors, our parents, and our house of worship.

A few of us may take issue with "trees and fields tell me nothing." But then we realize that our appreciation of nature's beauty was really taught and encouraged by our parents and teachers. We observe the glory of nature happening right before our eyes, but our understanding of life, growth, and death comes from our understanding of the teachings of people.

I will keep my mind open to learn so that I can
make as many gains in learning as are available to me.

Bitterness imprisons life;
love releases it.
— HARRY EMERSON FOSDICK

We sometimes waste far too much energy licking old wounds, nursing old hurts. Harboring bitterness only causes us pain. It folds all our feelings into a tight little package and keeps them hidden from sight.

Moving from bitter to loving feelings doesn't happen overnight, but it does happen when we nurture ourselves and open ourselves to others. Letting friends and family help is one way to begin. Soon we will remember how wonderful and unthreatening love feels. Outgoing, warm, and trusting feelings flow through us toward others. We can harness our love and use it for emotional recovery. Eventually, we are freed of unnecessary pain. We are learning once again to love in an unqualified way—and to love ourselves.

I do not need to be imprisoned by bitterness.
I can set myself free.

⌁ NOVEMBER 28 ⌁

Time deals gently only with those who take it gently.
—ANATOLE FRANCE

There have been times when we've taken our lives too seriously. For whatever reasons—family problems, money problems, health problems—we've let those concerns distort all the events of the day into sad or personally threatening experiences. When we've been preoccupied with negative thoughts, it's probably been difficult to see good possibilities.

Life magically becomes better, easier, when we take it gently in manageable segments. Problems may seem insurmountable if we insist on seeing them stretch into the coming months or years. But when we challenge ourselves to live in this day, the time treats us more gently by giving us a clearer picture of what we must deal with in this smaller segment of time.

Today, I will concentrate only on the things that must be dealt with in these twenty-four hours.

You should not hold back from making a start
because of fears about the future.
—LEWIS F. PRESNALL

Too often we fold up our dreams and set them aside because we can't envision success. The dream of a new business or of a new home or even of a self-improvement plan is easily discarded if we allow ourselves to think only of reasons why it won't work. "Not enough money," we decide. Or, "I don't have enough experience." Or—worse yet—"I won't succeed because I never have before."

We can become free to pursue our dreams when we realize that the future is not an enemy waiting to thwart our efforts. What our tomorrows hold quite often depends on the decisions and moves we make today. Right now, we can make a start. We can set aside—not our dreams—but our fears of an unfriendly future.

The choices I make today will affect
the quality of my future.

*It is in vain to say human beings ought to be
satisfied with tranquility: they must have action;
and they will make it if they cannot find it.*
—CHARLOTTE BRONTË

Tranquil: free from agitation; calm, peaceful. This we understand; this we desire. We surely want to have tranquil lives. Before chronic illness, we may have taken peace and tranquility for granted, for we were actively involved with the pursuit of life. Happiness and contentment came automatically along with the rest, with no conscious thought about it.

Before long we began to understand that if we wished to be tranquil, our minds and our bodies needed activity. Tranquility, that inner sense of calm, comes from contentment with how we are living our lives—and how actively we are living.

Tranquility will increase with my activity.

⎯ DECEMBER 1 ⎯

The wise man looks at death with honesty,
dignity and calm, recognizing that the tragedy
it brings is inherent in the great gift of life.
—CORLISS LAMONT

Chronic illness tends to heighten our awareness of the fragility of life. Some of us may even become concerned that due to poor health we may not live as long as we'd once expected.

To ease our fears, we may want to initiate a conversation with family members about dying. Since each one of us has personal ideas about how we would like our funeral handled—which hymns, who will say the eulogy, and where it should be held—it only makes sense to share that information with loved ones. Few people feel comfortable talking about the possibility of dying, but with a straightforward discussion we can, at least for a while, set aside our own anxieties.

I am comforted knowing my family
understands my fears and needs.

*Habituation is a falling asleep or fatiguing
of the sense of time; which explains why
young years pass slowly, while later life
flings itself faster and faster upon its course.*
— THOMAS MANN

Our routines can become so rote that we're unaware of making choices. Suddenly, we realize we haven't done many of the things that matter most to us. With this realization comes another: Sometimes making no choice is, in fact, a choice in itself. If we move through each day doing the same things, saying the same words, living a copy of the day before—we have chosen to live safely. But we may think, "I wish I had . . ."

We don't have to completely change our lives in order to make better choices for ourselves. All we have to do is see all the choices open to us.

*What and how I choose
makes every day different from the last.*

～ DECEMBER 3 ～

Happiness is not being pained in body
nor troubled in mind.
— Thomas Jefferson

Teenagers say it all the time: "Hey, mellow out! Chill!" These words may be alien to us, but we can listen to these somewhat flippant admonitions.

Perhaps we do get too tense at times during certain phases of our lives. Pain, anxiety, or stress can cause us to tighten our muscles, to brace our bodies against the impact of our medical problems. The tighter our bodies become, the less patient and kind we are to those we love.

To help ourselves "mellow out," we first have to identify the feelings associated with tenseness. We can calm down by taking deep, slow, cleansing breaths. Let's do ourselves a favor and learn to relax, to mellow out.

By learning to let my body rest and relax, I can
concentrate on keeping my mind free and untroubled.

~ DECEMBER 4 ~

A tragedy means always a man's struggles with
that which is stronger than man.
—G. K. CHESTERON

Once the diagnosis of a long-term illness is learned, some of us may use it as an excuse to be sad, morbid, sullen, unfeeling, and uncaring. These behaviors are all counterproductive to the fulfilling lives we want to lead.

Those of us who undergo a major health change may consider it a tragedy. It is; loss of good health is a frightening change. But to keep our personal problems hidden, to never reach out for help and support—that is the truest tragedy.

We can reach out to those who love us and extend our arms to our Higher Power. Rather than being bitter, we can involve ourselves in the lives of others and allow our personal tragedies to generate triumphs.

My faith in a Higher Power and my faith in myself
grow stronger each day.

Forgiveness is the answer to the child's dream of a miracle by which what is broken is made whole again, what is soiled is again made clean.
—DAG HAMMARSKJÖLD

We all may feel a measure of guilt when relationships deteriorate or friends become angry with each other. Sometimes it's not the people around us who are to blame; sometimes it really is our fault. We've misspoken or said harsh and unfeeling words to a friend.

We can't undo our mistakes or take back our words, but we can ask for forgiveness and try to make amends. We can forgive others when they have hurt us, knowing that forgiveness keeps our relationships whole.

I don't have to wait for forgiveness from others; I can make my amends first.

~ DECEMBER 6 ~

A leader is a dealer in hope.
— NAPOLEON BONAPARTE

A good leader doesn't always have the firmest hand or the most knowledge about a subject, but instead has the ability to develop hope and enthusiasm for success in others. Leading others often means being a role model; it means confidently marching forward, not pushing others from behind.

We all are leaders at one time or another. Raising children or working with others or nurturing relationships—all these tasks require leadership at times. Our health care also requires our leadership, and we find the most success when we lead with a hopeful spirit. That hope is reflected in our cooperation with the medical community, and it is also shown in our eagerness to live life fully and joyfully.

My hope, enthusiasm, and growth
help me and others deal with chronic illness.

⌐ DECEMBER 7 ⌐

Man adjusts to what he should not;
he is unable to adjust to what he should.
—JEAN TOOMER

Most teenagers love French fries, soda pop, and candy bars. We know that most fast food and sugar are bad for us—and so do teenagers—but many of us continue to munch on junk food.

Now that we have an adult's perspective, one would think that adjusting to new things or getting rid of bad habits would become easier. Not so! Adjusting to change is not easy, particularly when it involves our health.

One of the most difficult problems is maintaining a balance between dealing with the chronic problem and wanting to live without it. We learn, despite our resistance to change, that we can have an illness and can adjust—we can remain strong and happy.

I am confident of my ability to deal with my illness
and live a good life.

⌒ DECEMBER 8 ⌒

There are some remedies worse than the disease.
—PUBLILIUS SYRUS

Sometimes the very medicines prescribed to help us return to a more stable health situation can cause side effects that can be nearly intolerable. How ludicrous that a drug intended to help us shake off the exhaustion caused by a chronic health condition can cause fatigue. What a joke on us that a pill taken for arthritis, for example, has the potential to cause other medical problems.

Despite these side effects, we should not stop following dosage instructions until we talk with our doctors, who can help minimize the side effects. In this way we will gain one more foothold in the process of learning to live with our problems.

I'll try to keep communication lines open with my doctor to make it as easy as possible upon myself.

*To see the goal of life as "winning" forces us to see
other people as competitors, threats to our happiness.
For us to "win," they have to "lose."*
—Harold Kushner

Our thinking is healthier when we see our goals as individual accomplishments, not as outdoing someone else. Others don't have to get less or be less in order for us to feel good about ourselves.

Rather than, "I beat someone out of a job," we need to understand that it's not a contest, but a matter of placing the most qualified person in a new position. We all have different skills, and it is usually the skill, not the person, that is recognized or rewarded. The person who possesses the needed skill is not necessarily better, nicer, or more worthwhile—even when that person is us. In accepting that, we are better able to work toward our personal goals without fear of competition.

The only winning I pursue is meeting my goals.

DECEMBER 10

In these times one must write with one's life.
This is the challenge to all of us.
—Antoine de St. Exupery

When we were younger, many of us had a prescribed course of life—first school, a job, marriage, and then children. We never realized, and luckily so, that we would be dealt cards in a game we wouldn't want to play.

With the illnesses, sorrows, and pain have come joy, delight, and happiness. We would not have wanted to see into the future, but now that we are here, we want to live life as well as we are able. The need to deal as best we can with our burdens advances us toward positive actions and thoughts. What good or bad things happen to us do not determine a life's story as much as the choices we make. We can choose to be challenged. We can choose our directions.

Changes or improvements can begin today
with the decisions I make.

⌒ DECEMBER 11 ⌒

I've heard He works with broken people.
I am sick, hurting, broken.
I am waiting and willing now. . . .
—FLORA E. MEREDITH

Sometimes life can feel so hopeless. Pain, anxiety about health, and fear can plague our thoughts. Admitting things are out of our control can be so hard. It takes a tremendous amount of courage to admit that we need help. Giving ourselves over to the care of our Higher Power is frightening when we have become used to taking care of our own needs.

The hardest job is ours, though, for we must be willing to let go of the part of ourselves that is troubled, in order to become whole once again. We must be willing to let go in order to be helped.

I have made the hardest move and placed myself into the care of my Higher Power. Now I must wait.

Unreal is action without discipline,
charity without sympathy, ritual without devotion.
—BHAGAVAD-GITA

It's so easy to routinely go about our lives without examining our motives, without deciding why we do the things we do. We may have become so accustomed to reacting to what we think is expected of us that we rarely ponder what we expect of ourselves. At what point do we become willing to know ourselves?

Now may be the right moment to decide whether we act upon our own values, beliefs, and feelings, or whether we react to some vague sense of what others expect. By doing this, we might be surprised to discover that our charitable and spiritual actions do not change but they will become real because they are created by our inward sense of direction, discipline, love of others, and acceptance of self.

The things I say and do today
will be directed by what I expect of myself,
not by what I think others expect of me.

~ DECEMBER 13 ~

'Tis a lesson you should heed, Try, try again.
If at first you don't succeed, Try, try again.
—WILLIAM E. HICKSON

Our teachers told us to try again. Our parents reminded us to try again. And sometimes we even did try again! Usually it was something simple like recopying poorly written homework. We hardly realized then that we would be carrying that message with us into adulthood. It's often difficult to listen to good advice; it's even harder to accept it.

When we learn to reassess our goals, to reset priorities, and to be more realistic about where we are really headed, trying again begins to make more sense. Trying again doesn't always mean doing it over again. It can mean trying something entirely new. It can mean daring to change.

Trying again means I give myself room to grow.

∼ DECEMBER 14 ∼

I am just a heartbeat away from loneliness.
—LAURA PALMER

The holiday season can be difficult for anyone who has had a major life change. A person who has been widowed, has moved, or has had to deal with new physical limitations may become lonesome when each holiday, birthday, or anniversary rolls around.

We sometimes cause ourselves pain by isolating ourselves. We may feel that no one wants to share the holiday with us or that we don't wish to impose the inconvenience of illness upon friends.

By reminding ourselves of the meaning of these special days, we often find that we can move out of our isolation. Holidays and other occasions reaffirm the value of tradition, love, and family. These days compel us to remember our place within a welcoming circle of friends and family.

I can choose to reach out during the holidays—
or any day.

⏤ DECEMBER 15 ⏤

The greatest of faults, I should say,
is to be conscious of none.
—THOMAS CARLYLE

We really know that we are not perfect. We are, like everyone else, beings capable of millions of behaviors. We can develop a humble self-awareness that takes all of our pluses and minuses into account. When we examine ourselves gently, but honestly, we find ourselves in a position where we can correct our own faults and become more tolerant and accepting of the faults of others.

The unconditional love we give ourselves—and everyone we care for—isn't blind to imperfections; instead, it openly accepts strengths and weaknesses.

Today, my love of myself and others will be shown in
my tolerance of imperfections.

∾ DECEMBER 16 ∾

It is well that there is no one without a fault,
for he would not have a friend in the world.
—WILLIAM HAZLITT

As youngsters, we may have had doubts, just as we do now, about making new friends. We imposed unwritten rules upon ourselves as we sought out new friends. Will they like me? How do I approach them? Will we have enough to talk about?

These questions are again in our minds as we approach old and new relationships. We might worry that since we aren't always feeling happy and well, our friends might no longer value our company. This is not usually true, but it may take us a little while to pull away from fear and self-doubt and to make real efforts at making and maintaining our friendships.

Today, I will let my friends know
just how important they are to me.

⸱ DECEMBER 17 ⸱

Sadness flies on the wings of the morning
and out of the heart of darkness comes the light.
— JEAN GIRAUDOUX

Many people—not just the chronically ill—experience a sense of sadness or longing at this time of year. Perhaps the season stirs memories of carefree, happier times or, instead, of holidays long ago that were unhappy and without fantasy.

Knowing that this sadness is not uncommon can be comforting and so is knowing we can resist sadness. If we're unhappy with old traditions, we can introduce new ones. If we've isolated ourselves, we can join in some group activities. And if we're tired, we can give ourselves permission to say no and to have time alone. We might also examine our expectations and remember that special days are not copies of earlier ones. Each is new.

In the holidays ahead, I will continue
to do the things that have been special.
I will abandon any pattern that gives me no joy.

~ DECEMBER 18 ~

*The only limit to our realization of tomorrow
will be our doubts of today.
Let us move forward with strong and active faith.*
—Franklin Delano Roosevelt

Major changes in our lives may stun us—with delight or perhaps disbelief. After all, not all changes are negative. But when the change is negative, when illness is diagnosed or when pain pervades each day, we may begin to doubt our own inner resources. Once physically strong, we will have to dig deeper than ever to tap into our spiritual resources as well.

If we have doubts today, it may be because we are still locked into our physical selves. We are more than body, and it is our spirits that can be nourished by our caring Higher Power. Our value and importance are revealed by that care. Knowing this, we can move forward with our lives.

*I will look beyond my physical body for
a source of strength and care.*

Life is not merely living but living in health.
— Martial

Living in health may seem impossible for the chronically ill. After all, we reason, it's difficult to live in health if we are sick.

In fact, living in health is an old-fashioned term, almost like a benediction. These days we want to experience the wellness that goes beyond physical health by emphasizing emotional and spiritual health. For the first time we can allow ourselves the right to wellness despite physical illness.

Even with an ongoing illness, most of us don't have constant pain or discomfort. There are many times we enjoy ourselves. Playing cards, gardening, going for a walk, praying, meditating—these activities exercise all of our being—physically, emotionally, and spiritually.

I will consider my wellness, not illness, my life goal.

~ DECEMBER 20 ~

Change does not change tradition. It strengthens it.
Change is a challenge and an opportunity, not a threat.
— PRINCE PHILIP

At holiday times and anniversaries and birthdays, we may lament, "I can't entertain anymore. I just don't have the room. I don't have the strength either." Is what we are telling ourselves really true? Are our friends and family members so shallow that they come to our homes only for roast beef or turkey? Do we really have to give up the joy of having company?

Quickly we recognize the nonsense of such thoughts and cope with this situation in the same way we have with so many others—we change and we adapt. We can still welcome our loved ones into our homes. In the simpler meals and the casual atmosphere, our friends and family members will find what they have come for— assurance that we still value their company.

I will serve my guests as always—
with love and fellowship.

⌒ DECEMBER 21 ⌒

To know after absence the familiar
street and road and village and house
is to know again the satisfaction of home.
—HAL BORLAND

Home is a word that carries all kinds of meanings for us. For the majority, home has always been our anchor—the place where we can go even when we have had the worst possible of all days. Home usually means love, but it certainly means security and comfort.

As the years go by, we understand that home has little to do with a physical structure. It can be a tiny apartment or an elaborate mansion. Or—better still—it can be the special comfort and security we feel within ourselves. It is, after all, what we bring to it and to the people around us. Home is, and always has been, where our heart is.

My home acts as one of the roots of my life,
and it has all the qualities that I bring to it.

~ DECEMBER 22 ~

What's a joy to the one is a nightmare to the other.
That's how it is today, that's how it will be forever.
— BERTOLT BRECHT

Different strokes for different folks is a popular cliché, but it's also an absolute truth when it comes to knowing people. Each of us has our own level of comfort for the activities we do and the performances we give in our lives.

We also find different levels of joy in our spiritual, social, and emotional experiences. Often, we find what we're looking for—what we wish to find—in each situation. What's most important is that we are able to find our own level of joy—wherever we are at that time— and claim it as belonging to us.

My joy may not be the same as someone else's joy, but
I shall struggle on to keep the meaning of my joy alive.

*It is a great piece of skill to know how to
guide your luck even while waiting for it.*
—BALSTAR GRACIAN

Manipulation sounds like such a harsh word, but consider the hands of a surgeon, the moves of an artist, the skill of an electrician. They manipulate their physical environment. In doing so, they are creating. In some subtle way—perhaps we are not even aware that we are doing it—we learn to manipulate our lives. We, too, are very creative.

Some people are able to reach for positive goals, even during seemingly negative times. These people are capable of scooping out the very best of life. Those are the ones who have learned the delicate art of helping themselves. They can create their own luck.

*Sometimes luck isn't caused by a draw of the cards.
I work hard in all areas to improve my lot,
to improve my relationships, to improve my life.*

⏤ DECEMBER 24 ⏤

I have been sick and I have found out,
only then, how lonely I am. Is it too late?
—EUDORA WELTY

At one time, we may have thought in absolute terms. Either a person was our best friend or not. Things were right or wrong. We may have driven people from us—people we could have loved and who would have enriched our lives.

We have learned that if we are not happy, we need not accept things as they stand. The first step is always to admit there is a problem. Whether it's loneliness, or we have been too brusque with others, or we need a spiritual change, we can admit it and do whatever is necessary to improve. We can turn to friends or even professionals for help if we need it. We can do this because it's never too late.

Although the very thought of change is frightening,
I will assess my life and begin anew today.

*All living souls welcome whatsoever
they are ready to cope with. . . .*
— GEORGE SANTAYANA

So often, a problem would be overwhelming if we had to solve it all at once. We can allow ourselves to dwell only on small pieces of the problem at one time. Then, when we've come to terms with one part, another portion can be dealt with. Whether we are facing the death of a loved one or having to cope with other personal problems, our minds help us sort out the order in which we can best handle our pain.

Sometimes, we insist on tackling all of the problem, and we think ourselves into a kind of numbness. We're unable to act. At those times, perhaps we can remind ourselves of how our minds work best. If we do, we can let go of the whole situation and, instead, take on only the small part we're strong enough to handle.

*Today, I will let go of all I'm trying to cope with.
I will pick one or two small, positive things I can do.
Then, I will do them.*

Never let life's hardships disturb you. After all,
no one can avoid problems, not even saints or sages.
—NICHIREN DAISHONEN

A worry-free life. Wouldn't that be the ticket? It's hard to even imagine what life would be like with no problems. Once in a while a person will say, "If only I'd known . . . I never would have . . ." Or, "If I had understood . . . I should have . . ."

We can't live life always regretting past mistakes, and we shouldn't fear future ones either. The key to survival is not maintaining a stiff upper lip, as we have been told, but to express our vulnerability. Stoicism gets nothing but more stress, so we're learning to acknowledge our hardships as they come along. We're not complaining or whining. We're just bonding ourselves to the rest of the human race.

I can face new problems, not because I'm so strong,
but because I can honestly admit my weaknesses.

∼ DECEMBER 27 ∼

For age is opportunity no less
Than youth itself, though in
another dress,
And as evening twilight fades away
the sky is filled with stars,
invisible day.
— HENRY WADSWORTH LONGFELLOW

As young children, we probably had favorite elderly people who made us feel special. We never gave much thought to their age. During young adulthood, however, we may have begun to dread getting older. For some reason we saw the outward signs of aging as the beginning of the end.

As we become wiser and more mature, we come to realize that we once again venerate elderly people—for their wisdom, for their love, for their skills, and, especially, for their joy of living. Many of us seem to choose one or two special people whom we wish to be like. And then we try our hardest to measure up.

I look forward to the wisdom and joy of living
that often come with age. I am no longer afraid.

⌒ DECEMBER 28 ⌒

Sadness flies away on the wings of time.
—JEAN DE LA FONTAINE

When we're sad, it's hard to believe that time will heal all our wounds. An old family-practice doctor used to call it the TOT Treatment—Tincture of Time.

Our sadness may be due to a change in living patterns or even in the weather. It might be due to loss of a loved one, of good health, or even of a cherished object. And our grief takes time.

Whatever the reason for our sadness, after a self-imposed period of time alone, we begin to venture out once again into our world. We work our way, ever so slowly, back into some pattern of normalcy. TOT has done its work once again. Laughter surfaces, and we know we have put enough time and space between us and our sadness. We are whole again.

A time of sadness is natural,
just as natural as the rediscovered joy that follows it.

～ DECEMBER 29 ～

The proper function of man is to live, not to exist.
I shall not waste my days in trying to prolong them.
—JACK LONDON

We are on a remarkable journey that holds wonderful possibilities. Sometimes people who have undergone a crisis think they have arrived at the end of the journey. The excitement of living decreases each day.

Surrounding ourselves with loving, caring people gives us the greatest chance of coming out of the depression caused by our problems. Also, treating ourselves gently can improve our outlook. When we show loving care for others and ourselves, we will once again be moving back into the mainstream of life. We will be filled once again with the excitement and joy of the journey that lies ahead.

I owe myself the excitement of each day to come.
Today, I will savor my life.

To forgive is the highest, most beautiful form of love.
In return, you will receive untold peace and happiness.
—ROBERT MULLER

When we are trying to cope with a newly diagnosed illness, feelings may be hurt a little too easily, especially when we feel slighted by the very people we feel should understand. We probably are more vulnerable to hurt at first, and at times we may even feel sorry for ourselves.

There comes a time, however, when we can see the futility of carrying old grudges. There's no longer a need to know or prove who was right and who was wrong. As we've learned to cope with our illnesses, we've become emotionally stronger—strong enough to let go of anger and to forgive. The more we forgive, the calmer and more serene we will become, until ultimately our reward will be inner peace and trust.

I can let go of past hurts.
I can bridge the gap caused by misunderstandings.

~ DECEMBER 31 ~

*Afflictions are not really a good gift — neither they
nor their consequences. However, if afflictions do come,
it is well that we convert them into afflictions of love.
Herein lies the power of man.*
—CHAIM NACHMAN BIALIK

All around us we hear cries of "Happy New Year," and
we wonder if this next year is going to be happier than
last year was. Carrying the burden of chronic pain or a
chronic illness is far more demanding than most people
can imagine. It can overwhelm our days.

We alone have the power to convert that pain, loneliness, and any feelings of guilt into external expressions
of ourselves, such as helping others. It's almost impossible to be completely wound up in ourselves when we
are doing for others.

*I feel positive thoughts about this new year.
My goal is to reach out to at least one person each day.*

Peace rises like dawn in the hearts of hope. . . .
Peace reaches from warm and welcoming houses
  when workers go home.
Peace wraps congregations as worship comes to
  comforting conclusions. . . .
Peace floats like music through cabin windows to
  porch-sitters outside.
Peace shimmers from lake water on star-dashed
  extravagant nights. . . .
Peace blesses the day's end, in the Dylan Thomas way:
  "I turned the gas down. I got into bed. I said
  some words into the close and holy darkness, and
  then I slept."
And so the last page turns to the new page, and
  we wish the world a happy new year. In peace.

This excerpt is from an editorial written by Ann Daly Goodwin that appeared in the *St. Paul Pioneer Press* on December 31, 1986. Reprinted with permission.

INDEX

A

B

C

ABOUT THE AUTHOR

When Sefra Kobrin Pitzele developed a chronic illness, she dedicated her life to help others who are also dealing with health issues. Writing and public speaking quickly became her venues. Pitzele has written many books since then and will continue to do so.

Pitzele is involved in many activities, including being a member of the only women's Rotary in the United States. She enjoys going out with friends, volunteering, doing crafts, and seeing movies. She lives in Saint Paul, Minnesota.

vival remedy or the borrowing of a state survival statute.

Many Americans are employed by American-based employers to perform maritime work within the territorial waters of another nation. When one of these workers is killed, recovery by his representative or beneficiaries may turn, in part, upon whether the territorial waters are the "high seas" where DOHSA applies, or whether the general maritime common law, i.e., *Moragne* and *Gaudet*, applies. Most lower courts hold that DOHSA applies to death actions within the territorial waters of foreign sovereigns.

In the wrongful death action, the Jones Act beneficiaries take "by class"; the presence of a wife or child precludes recovery by the beneficiaries in the next lower class, the parents, and the presence of an eligible parent precludes recovery by any member of the next class, other dependent relatives. Under DOHSA, all of these beneficiaries are eligible to recover and share in the award, even though some would be in a higher "class" than others under the Jones Act approach. In applying *Moragne*, the lower courts have utilized the DOHSA approach and permit all of the beneficiaries to recover. One unresolved question is whether the more remote *Moragne* beneficiaries, such as parents or siblings, must have been financially dependent upon the victim at death. The Jones Act and DOHSA demand that these relatives be "dependent," a logical requirement inasmuch as those acts permit recovery of pecuniary benefits only. If *Moragne* permits recovery of nonpecuniary benefits, such as loss of society, the requirement of beneficiary dependency would be a matter of policy, not logic. The weight of authority is that parents and siblings cannot recover under *Moragne* unless they were dependent on the victim. *See Sutton v. Earles* (9th Cir.1994), and the cases cited therein.

Under all three wrongful death actions—Jones Act, DOHSA and *Moragne*—the personal representative is the proper party plaintiff and controls the litigation, unless there is a conflict of interest between the representative and the beneficiaries. *See Calton v. Zapata Lexington* (5th Cir.1987), and the authorities cited therein. State law furnishes the rule for determining whether a claimant has the requisite legal relationship with the victim to qualify as a beneficiary in the wrongful death action. *Tidewater Marine Towing, Inc. v. Curran–Houston, Inc.* (5th Cir.1986).

Formerly, the three maritime theories for wrongful death recovery were time-barred by different standards. The Jones Act was subject to a three-year statute of limitations, DOHSA had a two-year statute of limitations, and the common law remedy was governed by laches. The maritime tort personal injury and death statute of limitations, 46 U.S.C.A. § 763a, makes both DOHSA and the common law death actions subject to the same three-year limitation period as Jones Act claims.

A Jones Act death claim may be brought in federal court at law or in admiralty or in state court. A death action premised upon *Moragne* may be brought in admiralty or in state court or, if there is diversity jurisdiction, on the law side of federal court. DOHSA, 46 U.S.C.A. § 761, authorizes the personal representative of the decedent to bring an action "in the district courts of the United States, in admiralty." This language has led some courts to conclude that jurisdiction over a DOHSA claim is exclusively in the federal court sitting in admiralty, and the claimant is not entitled to trial by jury unless the claim is properly joined with some other claim (such as a Jones Act claim) triable to a jury. Later decisions, including strong dicta by the Supreme Court in *Offshore Logistics, Inc. v. Tallentire*, page 311, *supra*, indicate that jurisdiction over a DOHSA claim is concurrent between the admiralty court and state court.

The Longshore and Harbor Workers' Compensation Act provides death benefits to designated beneficiaries if the work-related injury causes death, or if an employee who is permanently disabled in a compensable accident dies thereafter from other causes. 33 U.S.C.A. § 909. It also provides for survival of a claim for permanent partial disability where the employee dies from causes other than the work-related injury. 33 U.S.C.A. § 908(d)(1). The extension of survival benefits when the death is not related to the compensable injury was effected in the 1972 amendments to the LHWCA. Courts have held that these survival benefits are payable even though the compensable injury occurred prior to the effective date of the amendment. *See, e.g., Puig v.*

Standard Dredging Corp. (1st Cir.1979), and the
cases cited therein. Benefits payable to disabled
workers under the LHWCA are subject to a maxi-
mum "ceiling" of 200% of the national average
weekly wage of production or nonsupervisory workers on private, nonagricultural payrolls. Construing
the 1972 amendments, the United States Supreme
Court held that the "ceiling" did not apply to death
benefits payable under the Act. *Director, Office of
Workers' Compensation Programs v. Rasmussen*
(S.Ct.1979). However, a 1984 amendment imposes
the 200% "ceiling" on death benefits. 33 U.S.C.A.
§ 909(e).

CHAPTER XV

PLATFORM INJURIES

A. HISTORY AND BACKGROUND

Exploration for minerals beneath navigable waters is conducted from movable drilling structures or from stationary platforms constructed over water and permanently attached to the subsoil and seabed. Maritime law treats the movable structures as vessels, and thus within admiralty jurisdiction, even when the structures are temporarily attached to the seabed. The stationary or "fixed" platforms, however, are treated as land, *see Rodrigue v. Aetna Cas. & Surety Co.* (S.Ct.1969). The large number of accidents occurring on these stationary platforms has led to the development of a unique body of law which is intertwined with maritime personal injury law.

A little history aids a proper understanding of platform law. When exploration for minerals under the beds of navigable waters became feasible about the middle of the twentieth century, the United States, first by presidential proclamation and later by international convention, obtained ownership and dominion over the natural resources in the seabed and subsoil of the Continental Shelf, which in some areas extends as much as two hundred miles seaward from the American coastline. The United States Supreme Court thereafter held that all of the Shelf and its resources, from the coastline seaward, belonged to the federal sovereign. *United States v. California* (S.Ct.1947). Subsequently, Congress ceded to each coastal state the lands beneath that state's territorial waters, i.e., those waters lying within the projection seaward of the state's boundaries for designated distances. 43 U.S.C.A. §§ 1301, 1311. Those statutes have been interpreted as extending the dominion of the states of Texas and Florida seaward a distance of three marine leagues (about nine geographical miles) and the boundaries of Louisiana, Mississippi and Alabama seaward a distance of three geographical miles. *See United States v. Louisiana, Texas, Mississippi, Alabama and Florida* (S.Ct.1960); *United States v. Florida* (S.Ct.1975). For the remainder of the Shelf (the Outer Continental Shelf), Congress provided:

> To the extent that they are applicable and not inconsistent with this subchapter or with other Federal laws and regulations ... now in effect or hereafter adopted the civil and criminal laws of each adjacent State ... are declared to be the law of the United States for that portion of the ... outer Continental Shelf ... which would be within the area of the state if its boundaries were extended seaward to the outer margin of the outer Continental Shelf.... 43 U.S.C.A. § 1333(a)(2)(A).

Thus if there is no applicable federal law: (1) state law applies on the Outer Continental Shelf as "surrogate" federal law, and (2) state law applies of its own force within the state's territorial waters. The difference may be more than semantic. When federal law preempts state law under the Supremacy Clause (such as within a state's territorial waters), subsequently developing federal common law presumably takes precedence over state law. The result may not be the same if federal common law develops after Congress adopted state law in the Outer Shelf Lands Act, since arguably the effect in such case would be to give federal common law priority over a federal statute. The Supreme Court alluded to but did not squarely face this intriguing question in *Gulf Offshore Co. v. Mobil Oil Corp.* (S.Ct.1981).

B. TORT CLAIMS

If a platform is located on the Outer Continental Shelf, state tort law applies as "surrogate" federal law, unless there is applicable federal law. If the platform is within territorial waters, state tort law applies unless it is preempted by applicable federal law. Thus torts occurring on platforms ordinarily will be governed by state law unless there is some applicable federal law. One such law is the Admiralty Extension Act, which applies only if the tort was "caused by a vessel on navigable waters" and has "maritime flavor." However, the AEA frequently will not apply to the platform injury because the accident is not due to a defect in an appurtenance of the vessel but is caused by personnel performing service for the vessel. *Dahlen v. Gulf Crews, Inc.*

(5th Cir.2002). Similarly, a wrongful death occurring in connection with a platform may fall under the Death on the High Seas Act, if the wrongful act occurs on the high seas and, perhaps, has "maritime flavor." (*See* Chapter XIV, *supra*). Otherwise, torts occurring on a platform ordinarily do not fall within maritime tort jurisdiction since the maritime common law treats the platform as an "extension of the land" (and thus lacking in "locality") and deems exploration for oil and gas from fixed platforms as lacking in "maritime flavor." *Rodrigue v. Aetna Cas. & Surety Co.* (S.Ct.1969); *Herb's Welding, Inc. v. Gray,* page 260, *supra.* The same result may attain when an injury occurs on the water near a platform because of negligence in the platform drilling process; there is "locality," but "flavor" may be lacking. *See, e.g., In re Dearborn Marine Service, Inc.* (5th Cir.1974). Accordingly, state law usually governs the resolution of tort claims that arise from activities on fixed platforms. When state law governs, the litigants take that law in its entirety, including a state statute of limitations which may be shorter than the federal maritime statute, 46 U.S.C.A. § 763a, or that provides a time bar different from that which would result through application of the maritime doctrine of laches. *Chevron Oil Co. v. Huson* (S.Ct.1971).

State tort law may not apply to all non-maritime torts that occur on fixed platforms. There are numerous federal regulations governing safety on platforms, and many accidents occurring on the platforms are caused at least in part by violation of those regulations. Prior to 1978, the federal courts refused to imply a federal cause of action for damages from a violation of such regulations. In that year, however, the Outer Continental Shelf Lands Act (OCSLA) was amended to provide:

It shall be the duty of any holder of a lease or permit . . . to

(1) Maintain all places of employment within the lease area . . . in compliance with occupational safety and health standards and . . . free from recognized hazards to employees . . . [and]

(2) maintain all operations . . . in compliance with regulations intended to protect persons . . . on the Outer Continental Shelf . . . 43 U.S.C.A. § 1348(b)

and

Any resident of the United States who is injured in any manner through the failure of any operator to comply with any rule, regulation, order, or permit issued pursuant to this subchapter may bring an action for damages [including reasonable attorney and expert witness fees] only in the judicial district having jurisdiction under paragraph (1) of this subsection. 43 U.S.C.A. § 1349(b)(2).

Arguably, these provisions establish a federal statutory action for damages caused by unsafe conditions or the violation of federal safety regulations on platforms located on the Shelf. This view has yet to find judicial support. *See, e.g., Wentz v. Kerr–McGee*

Corp. (5th Cir.1986). Even if the amendments did not create a new federal cause of action, a stronger argument now can be made that a federal cause of action should be implied from violation of the duties imposed upon lease holders by the provisions of the Outer Continental Shelf Lands Act and by regulations adopted pursuant to the Act. Applying the test provided by the Supreme Court in *Cort v. Ash* (S.Ct.1975) to the original version of the OCSLA, the Fifth Circuit concluded that a federal damage action for maritime workers could not be implied. *Olsen v. Shell Oil Co.* (5th Cir.1977). However, the 1977 amendments added the provisions cited above and other sections which reflect a strong Congressional purpose of promoting the safety of workers on the Shelf, an important ingredient in the *Cort* test for implying the existence of a federal cause of action.

Federal and state courts have concurrent jurisdiction over claims arising on the Outer Continental Shelf. *Gulf Offshore Co. v. Mobil Oil Corp.*, page 323, *supra*. Venue is proper "in the judicial district in which any defendant resides or may be found, or in the judicial district of the State nearest the place the cause of action arose." 43 U.S.C.A. § 1349(b)(1).

Drilling operations on an offshore platform usually are conducted by contractors and specialized subcontractors. This presents nice legal questions such as the duty which the platform owner or operator owes to the contractor's employees. The owner or operator may not owe a duty to persons on the platform unless it has "operational control" over the contractor's work or expressly or impliedly approves the contractor's unsafe work practice. *Fruge v. Parker Drilling Co.* (5th Cir.2003).

Another interesting issue is whether the contractor's immunity from workplace negligence through worker compensation extends to the platform owner or operator. The most frequently litigated issue is indemnification. The contracts for drilling operations on an offshore platform commonly contain indemnity agreements. Maritime law upholds the validity of an indemnity agreement in which the indemnitor agrees to indemnify against indemnitee negligence, but some of the oil producing states, such as Texas and Louisiana, have adopted statutes which invalidate indemnitee-negligence provisions in mineral exploration contracts. Thus determination of the validity of the indemnity provision in a platform operations contract may turn upon whether the contract is maritime. *See, e.g., Smith v. Penrod Drilling Corp.* (5th Cir.1992). Some indemnitee-negligence agreements for operations on the Outer Continental Shelf are validated by 33 U.S.C.A. § 905(c), which expressly authorizes "reciprocal" indemnity agreements between a vessel owner and the maritime employer of a worker who is covered by the LHWCA through the OCSLA.

The general rule is that the state law designated by the Outer Continental Shelf Lands Act applies, even though that state's choice of law rules would dictate the application of the law of a sister state.

C. WORKER'S COMPENSATION CLAIMS

Workers on movable drilling structures on navigable waters may qualify as seamen under the prevailing test for seaman status. *See* Chapter XIII. If a worker qualifies as a seaman, his claim against his employer is not affected by the fact that his injury occurs on a fixed platform. A seaman's recovery under the Jones Act and for maintenance and cure is not limited to accidents occurring on water, and in some situations, a seaman may recover damages from the vessel for injuries occurring on land but caused by an unseaworthy condition of the vessel.

If the exploration for minerals is conducted from a fixed platform as opposed to a movable rig which qualifies as a vessel, a worker ordinarily will not attain seaman status. A seaman must have the requisite connexity with a vessel, and in maritime law a fixed platform is land, not a vessel. Some workers on fixed platforms may qualify as seamen because of their relationship to a vessel used in support of the platform's drilling activities. However, those craft ordinarily serve merely as "floating hotels" for the workers, and only cooks and others who perform much of their duties aboard the support vessel will qualify as seamen. A non-seaman on a "jack up" rig jacked up on the OCS may be covered by the LHWCA if the rig is treated as a "device ... temporarily attached to the seabed." *Demette v. Falcon Drilling Co.* (5th Cir.2002).

Claims against employers by non-seamen working on fixed platforms will be governed by the LHWCA or by state worker's compensation, depending upon the geographical area in which the injury occurs. The OCSLA provides:

> With respect to disability or death of an employee resulting from an injury occurring as the result of operations conducted on the outer Continental Shelf for the purpose of exploring for, developing, removing or transporting by pipeline the natural resources, or involving rights to the natural resources, of the subsoil and seabed of the outer Continental Shelf, compensation shall be payable under the provisions of the Longshoremen's and Harbor Workers' Compensation Act. For the purposes of the extension of the provisions of the [LHWCA] under this section—(1) the term "employee" does not include a master or member of a crew of any vessel, or an officer or employee of the United States or of any State.... 43 U.S.C.A. § 1333(b)

The Act clearly covers the compensation claims of privately-employed non-seamen injured while working on platforms on the Outer Continental Shelf. It also may extend the benefits of the LHWCA to some workers injured in accidents within territorial and inland waters and on land; section 1333(b) does not expressly require that the injury occur on the Outer Continental Shelf, but only that the injury "occur ... as a result of operations conducted" on the Shelf. There is a split of authority on whether LHWCA coverage applies under Section 1333(b) only if the worker suffers injury on the Shelf. *Compare Mills v. Director, Office of Workers' Compensation Programs* (5th Cir.1989), and *Curtis v. Schlumberger Offshore Service, Inc.* (3d Cir.1988).

May a worker injured on a platform on the Outer Continental Shelf claim benefits under a state worker's compensation statute? Many of the state statutes extend coverage to workers injured outside the state, if the contract of employment is made within the state. One state Supreme Court has held that the adoption by the OCSLA of the LHWCA does not preclude application of state worker's compensation laws to injuries occurring on platforms on the Shelf. *Thompson v. Teledyne Movible Offshore, Inc.* (La.1982). However, federal court decisions have cast doubt upon the validity of that holding. *See, e.g., LeSassier v. Chevron, USA Inc.* (5th Cir. 1985); *Gates v. Shell Oil Co.* (5th Cir.1987).

The claim of a worker against his employer for injury on a fixed platform within territorial or inland waters usually is governed by the applicable state worker's compensation law, since (1) the worker usually does not qualify as a seaman, (2) he is not within the coverage of the LHWCA through the OCSLA, and (3) he usually lacks "status" as a maritime worker under the LHWCA. *Herb's Welding Inc. v. Gray,* page 260, *supra*, or is not injured on a covered situs. *Thibodeaux v. Grasso Prod. Mgmt., Inc.* (5th Cir.2004). *Herb's Welding*, however, may not preclude LHWCA coverage for a mineral exploration platform worker who spends some of his time in "indisputable longshoring operations," such as loading and unloading vessels supplying the platform.

Foreign workers on fixed platforms off the shores of foreign sovereigns generally will be precluded from coverage under the Jones Act or the LHWCA, either by statutory exclusion, (*see* 46 U.S.C. § 688b and 33 U.S.C. § 688(b) and Chapter XIII, *supra*) or because they do not otherwise meet the requirements for such coverage. American workers on fixed platforms in foreign waters may qualify as seamen but probably do not meet the "situs" requirement (injury on navigable waters of the United States) of the LHWCA. Their remedy often is through the worker compensation scheme of an American state with close ties to the worker or his employment contract.

CHAPTER XVI

SOVEREIGN IMMUNITY

Prior to 1916, the doctrine of sovereign immunity barred suits against the United States on maritime claims. In that year, in the Shipping Act, Congress made a limited waiver of immunity; however, the waiver permitted the arrest *in rem* of vessels under federal control, and for that reason proved unsatisfactory. In 1919 Congress adopted the Suits in Admiralty Act (SIAA), 46 U.S.C.A. § 741 et seq., which authorized suits *in personam* against the United States for damages caused by a "merchant vessel" owned by the United States, but prohibited arrest or seizure of the vessel. If a claim did not fit within the Suits in Admiralty Act, such as where the vessel was a warship, the claimant was required to seek special legislation authorizing an action against the sovereign. In 1925, Congress adopted the Public Vessels Act, 46 U.S.C.A. § 781 et seq., which permits actions *in personam* against the United States for torts committed by "public vessels," including warships.

This disjointed approach to the waiver of sovereign immunity resulted in one hiatus: a ship under federal control which was neither a "merchant vessel" nor a "public vessel" did not come within the waiver of immunity in either statute. To eliminate

332

this loophole, Congress in 1960 amended the Suits in Admiralty Act to extend the waiver of immunity to all cases "where if such vessel were privately owned or operated . . . or if a private person or property were involved, a proceeding in admiralty could be maintained." This raised another issue: since the 1960 amendment placed all vessels under federal control within the language of the SIAA, did that act supersede the Public Vessels Act? The issue is not one of great significance, since the acts contain many similar provisions (including prohibitions against *in rem* proceedings, provisions permitting the sovereign to limit liability, and authorizations for arbitration or compromise of claims) and only a few differences (the SIAA provides more liberal venue rules, permits prejudgment interest and does not require "reciprocity" in suits brought by foreign nationals). The Supreme Court answered the question in the negative in *United States v. United Continental Tuna Corp.* (S.Ct.1976). Thus if a tort is committed by a vessel belonging to the United States but not engaged in trade or commerce (such as a warship, customs patrol boat, Coast Guard search and rescue boat, or Army Corps of Engineers utility boat), the waiver of sovereign immunity is governed by the Public Vessels Act, to the extent its provisions differ from the Suits in Admiralty Act.

A more important and as yet unresolved issue is whether the Suits in Admiralty Act applies to maritime but non-vessel negligent acts of the federal sovereign. In 1946, Congress made a general waiver of tort immunity through the Federal Tort Claims

Act (FTCA), now 28 U.S.C.A. § 2671 et seq. From 1946 until the 1960 amendment to the Suits in Admiralty Act, maritime tort claims against the United States which were not caused by a vessel, either "merchant" or "public," were brought under the FTCA. The 1960 amendment to the Suits in Admiralty Act, however, can be read as encompassing all maritime tort claims against the federal sovereign, including non-vessel torts which between 1946 and 1960 were brought under the FTCA. The lower courts generally hold the SIAA and PVA now preempt the FTCA in all maritime torts claims against the federal sovereign. *McCormick v. United States* (5th Cir.1982); *Kelly v. United States* (2d Cir.1976). *Compare Jones & Laughlin Steel, Inc. v. Mon River Towing, Inc.* (3d Cir.1985). The issue is significant, since there are important differences between the Suits in Admiralty Act and the FTCA, such as the pre-suit procedures, the courts in which they may be brought, the standards for liability and the statutes of limitations. The FTCA specifically provides a "discretionary function exception," *i.e.*, the sovereign is not liable for errors in performance of, or for failure to perform a discretionary function or duty. *See, e.g., Dalehite v. United States* (S.Ct. 1953). The SIAA does not explicitly provide such an exception to sovereign liability, although the courts have read it into the act. *See, e.g., McMellon v. United States* (4th Cir.2004).

When the waiver of immunity applies, the federal government is liable in the same manner as a private party, except that an *in rem* action may not be maintained. The SIAA has a two-year time limitation for filing of suit; the majority view is that it is a peremptory period or statute or repose, and not a statute of limitations; thus it is not subject to tolling or waiver. 46 U.S.C.A. § 745. *But see McCormick v. United States* (5th Cir.1982). Under the FTCA, filing an administrative claim (which is required) tolls the statute of limitations. In contrast, the submission of an administrative claim is not a prerequisite to bringing suit under the SIAA, and therefore the act does not provide for the tolling of the two-year period upon the filing of a claim with an administrative body. Thus, if a plaintiff with a maritime tort claim against the government mistakenly files an administrative claim but does not file a suit within two years, the claim will be time barred. *See, e.g., Williams v. United States* (9th Cir.1983). *Taghadomi v. United States* (9th Cir.2005). Recently, a court has held that the two year statute may be subject to equitable tolling. *Hedges v. United States* (3d Cir.2005). Another trap for the unwary may arise from the operation of the Admiralty Extension Act, 46 U.S.C. § 740(b), which provides that in AEA suits against the United States, the plaintiff must present a written claim, and then wait six months before filing suit. Thus, in one case, the claim to the agency owning or operating the injury causing vessel was made *less than* six months before the expiration of the two year statute of limitations. Consequently, the plaintiff could *not* wait six months *and* file his claim within two years; thus the claim was time barred. *Anderson v. United States* (11th Cir.2003).

Federal employees sustaining injuries in a maritime setting usually are relegated to proceedings against their employer under the Federal Employees Compensation Act, 5 U.S.C.A. § 8101 et seq.; 33 U.S.C. A. § 903(B).

The immunity of foreign states from maritime (and non-maritime) claims in American courts is governed by the Foreign Sovereign Immunities Act, adopted in 1976. The act provides sovereign immunity for claims arising out of noncommercial activities, but does not provide immunity for claims based upon commercial activities carried on in, or having a direct effect in the United States, or to acts performed in this country in connection with commercial activity elsewhere. 28 U.S.C.A. § 1604 et seq. The Act permits foreclosure upon a maritime lien *in personam* but does not permit an *in rem* proceeding against a vessel under the control of a foreign sovereign. 28 U.S.C.A. § 1605. A claimant may not obtain trial by jury against a foreign sovereign, even though he would otherwise be entitled to jury trial under federal maritime law. 28 U.S.C.A. § 1330. Jurisdiction over claims against foreign sovereigns is concurrent between federal and state courts, 28 U.S.C.A. § 1330, but a foreign sovereign may remove to federal court any civil action brought against it in a state court. 28 U.S.C.A. § 1441(d). There are special provisions for venue of such actions, 28 U.S.C.A. § 1391(f), and for the exercise of "long arm" jurisdiction over foreign sovereigns. 28 U.S.C.A. § 1608.

A state's immunity from suit in federal court, provided by the Eleventh Amendment, extends to maritime claims. *In re New York* (S.Ct.1921). A state may expressly waive the immunity by statute. It also may waive the immunity if it voluntarily invokes or clearly declares that it intends to submit itself to the jurisdiction of the federal court. However, a state does not impliedly waive its immunity from suit in federal court by participating in a maritime matter, even where there is an unambiguous statement of Congressional intent to subject the state to suit. *College Sav. Bank v. Florida Prepaid Postsecondary Edu. Expense Bd.* (S.Ct.1999). Congress also may not subject a nonconsenting state to some private suits for damages in the state's own courts. *Alden v. Maine* (S.Ct.1999). *Compare, State of Tennessee v. Lane* (S.Ct.2004). At least one court has held that the Eleventh Amendment does not shield a state from federal jurisdiction where the state seeks recovery of damages caused by a shipping accident when the shipowner has sought limitation of liability in federal court. *Magnolia Marine Transp. Co. v. Oklahoma* (10th Cir.2004).

Some political subdivisions and departments perform such functions, and their finances are so intertwined with the general state treasury, that they fall under the umbrella of the state's sovereign immunity under the Eleventh Amendment. The immunity of lesser governmental bodies probably will be determined by application of the general tort law governing immunity.

CHAPTER XVII

JOINT AND SEVERAL LIABIL-ITY, INDEMNITY AND CONTRIBUTION

Maritime tort law imposes joint and several liability upon joint tortfeasors. *Norfolk & Western Rwy. Co. v. Ayers* (S.Ct.2003); *Edmonds v. Compagnie Generale Transatlantique* (S.Ct.1979); *Coats v. Penrod Drilling Corp.* (5th Cir.1995).

However, there has been a radical shift in American law regarding joint and several liability in tort cases. Once the clear majority rule was that joint tortfeasors (tortfeasors who caused indivisible injuries) were jointly and severally liable. However, many jurisdictions, either through legislative enactment or judicial decision, have moved toward several or modified several liability for joint tortfeasors. While state law has moved away from joint and several liability, maritime law has held the traditional course, preserving joint and several liability. Consequently, maritime law may be quite appealing to the plaintiff seeking full recovery. Maritime law is even more appealing when one considers the holding of *Grubart, see* Chapter III, *supra*, that admiralty jurisdiction over a maritime joint tortfeasor will also provide maritime jurisdiction over a land based joint tortfeasor. This raises the interest-ing possibility that the land based joint tortfeasor may be exposed to joint and several liability under maritime law even though otherwise applicable state law may no longer recognize joint and several liability.

Where one person may be jointly and severally liable with another, issues of indemnification and contribution may arise. Liability for indemnity or contribution may arise because of a contract be-tween the parties or it may be arise in tort.

When the underlying obligation is maritime, ad-miralty law determines the extent to which a debtor who pays the creditor can shift all or part of the loss to a third person. Generally, an indemnification clause in a contract to unload a vessel is governed by admiralty law, since the underlying contract is maritime, but an indemnification provision in a shipbuilding contract is regulated by state law be-cause an agreement to construct a vessel is nonmar-itime. Similarly, tort indemnification and contribu-tion generally are governed by admiralty law if the underlying tort is maritime.

When the indemnity claim arises out of contract, the primary role of the law is to provide interpreta-tion and enforcement of the agreement. Some mari-time contractual indemnity provisions are invalid. The United States Supreme Court has ruled that an agreement by which a tow agrees to indemnify a tug from damages caused by the latter's negligence is invalid. *Bisso v. Inland Waterways Corp.* (S.Ct.

1955). The Longshore and Harbor Workers' Compensation Act, 33 U.S.C.A. § 905(b), invalidates any agreement by which an LHWCA employer agrees to indemnify the vessel owner for payment of damages to the employer's LHWCA employee, except for certain mutual indemnity agreements governing activities on the Outer Continental Shelf. 33 U.S.C.A. § 905(c).

Maritime law will enforce a contractual provision by which the indemnitor agrees to indemnify against the indemnitee's negligence, if the intent to do so is unequivocal. *See, e.g.*, *Roberts v. Williams–McWilliams Co.* (5th Cir.1981). Thus state laws which invalidate indemnity—negligence provisions in contracts involving mineral exploration have increased the importance of distinguishing between maritime and non-maritime contracts for offshore mineral development. *See, e.g., Smith v. Penrod Drilling Corp.* (5th Cir.1992). *See also,* Chapter III, *supra.*

Maritime law also has recognized an implied contractual indemnity, as an outgrowth of the *Sieracki* seaman doctrine. *See* page 279, *supra.* Prior to the 1972 amendments to the LHWCA, a longshoreman employed by a stevedore could recover damages from the vessel owner caused by an unseaworthy condition of the vessel, even though the condition was caused by the stevedore's negligence. In *Ryan Stevedoring Co., Inc. v. Pan–Atlantic Steamship Corp.* (S.Ct.1956), the Supreme Court provided the vessel owner with a remedy over against the stevedore in such a case. The Court ruled that a stevedore impliedly warranted that it would perform its services in a workmanlike manner; if breach of that warranty caused the vessel owner damage, such as the damages it was required to pay to the longshoreman for the injuries caused by the unseaworthy condition, the vessel owner could recover indemnification from the stevedore. However, the circumstances which gave rise to this *Ryan* doctrine changed in 1972, when Congress substituted a negligence action, 905(b), for the maritime employee's unseaworthiness remedy against the vessel, and also provided that the maritime employer was not liable to the vessel owner for the employee's damages, either "directly or indirectly," and that "any agreements or warranties to the contrary shall be void." 33 U.S.C.A. § 905(b).

The warranty of workmanlike performance in maritime law grew out of the *Sieracki* and *Ryan* doctrines; after their demise, its status remains uncertain. *See Fontenot v. Mesa Petroleum Co.* (5th Cir.1986), *Bosnor, S.A. de C.V. v. Tug L.A. Barrios* (5th Cir.1986). *See also*, Chapter XI. Some courts have held that the warranty extends to all contracts for the performance of maritime services, while others have limited its application to stevedoring contracts. The importance of the survival of the warranty of workmanlike performance depends primarily upon whether it imposes upon the maritime contractor a duty more onerous than reasonable care.

Tort indemnification in maritime law may arise when the indemnitor's negligence "triggers" the indemnitee's liability (such as vicarious liability, or a shipowner's absolute liability for an unseaworthy condition or for maintenance and cure). *See, e.g., Federal Marine Terminals, Inc. v. Burnside Shipping Co., Ltd.* (S.Ct.1969). Before the advent of comparative contribution, maritime law also provided tort indemnification when the negligence of one joint tortfeasor was "slight" and that of another was "gross." After adoption of contribution between joint tortfeasors on the basis of percentages of fault, indemnification under the "gross-slight" rule appears to serve no useful purpose and may no longer exist in maritime law. *See, e.g., Loose v. Offshore Navigation, Inc.* (5th Cir.1982).

Where two or more defendants are at fault, contribution ordinarily applies. Where the liability of one is based upon a "no-fault" theory (such as, arguably, unseaworthiness), the faulty tortfeasor may not be entitled to contribution (although the non faulty defendant may be entitled to indemnity, as discussed above). *See, e.g., Cooper Stevedoring Co., Inc. v. Fritz Kopke, Inc.* (S.Ct.1974).

Initially, admiralty law enforced contribution among joint tortfeasors only in collision cases; if two or more vessels were at fault, the damages were divided equally between or among them. *The Catharine: Lewis v. Dickinson* (S.Ct.1855). In other cases, maritime law generally followed the common law rule barring contribution among joint tortfeasors, although the rule was not always followed by lower courts. The case often cited for the proposition that admiralty law did not permit contribution in non-collision cases was *Halcyon Lines v. Haenn Ship Ceiling & Refitting Corp.* (S.Ct.1952), in which a vessel owner was denied contribution from a ship repairer for damages paid to the repairer's employee. In *Cooper Stevedoring Co., Inc. v. Fritz Kopke, Inc.,* page 342, *supra,* the Supreme Court, reviewing the jurisprudence, declared that there was a "well-established maritime rule allowing contribution between joint tortfeasors." *Halcyon,* the Court noted, did not support the opposing view, but merely represented an exception to the rule: contribution may not be enforced against a negligent party who is immune from tort liability to the victim, such as in *Halcyon,* where the maritime employee's exclusive remedy against his employer was the compensation benefits provided by the Longshore and Harbor Workers' Compensation Act.

The Court's opinion in the *Cooper Stevedoring Co.* case left open the question of whether contribution should be made on a per capita basis, as in the rule of divided damages, or on a percentage basis, which would be more harmonious with the maritime rule of "pure" comparative negligence. Subsequently, the Court swept away the rule of "divided damages," holding that contribution in collision cases must be made on the basis of the percentage of fault of the offending vessels. *United States v. Reliable Transfer Co., Inc.* (S.Ct.1975). Since that decision, the courts uniformly hold that contribution in non-collision cases also is on the basis of percentages of fault.

A victim's settlement of a maritime claim with less than all of the tortfeasors presents problems at sea and on land. The settlement may not discharge the non-settling tortfeasors, since the release of a co-debtor does not discharge other co-debtors unless the parties intend such as a result. *Cates v. United States* (5th Cir.1971). The settlement does defeat the non-settling tortfeasor's right to contribution from the settling tortfeasor, but the victim's recovery against the non-settling tortfeasor is reduced by the percentage of fault assessed to the settling tortfeasor. *McDermott, Inc. v. AmClyde and River Don Castings Ltd.* (S.Ct.1994). There is scant authority for the proposition that where the liability of the defendants is based not on negligence but on some theory of strict liability, the defendants are not joint tortfeasors; thus where the plaintiff settles with one of the defendants, its recovery against the other is not reduced by the percentage of fault allocated to the settling tortfeasor but by the dollar amount of the settlement. *Chisholm v. UHP Projects* (4th Cir.2000). The decision seems contrary to the spirit of *McDermott*.

May a party entitled to indemnity or contribution recover his costs, including attorney's fees incurred in defense of the victim's claim, from the party paying the indemnity or contribution? In cases involving implied contractual indemnity or tort indemnity, the courts have answered the question in the affirmative; the opposite result has been reached in contribution cases.

CHAPTER XVIII

LIMITATION OF LIABILITY

A. GENERALLY

When a voyage or event subjects the owner of a vessel to liability, maritime law sometimes permits him to limit his liability arising out of the voyage or event to the value of his vessel (and "freight then pending") at the conclusion of the voyage or event. This remedy, called limitation of liability, is found in the maritime law of many nations, and was adopted by Congress as part of American admiralty law in the mid-nineteenth century.

In addition to limiting liability, limitation also permits the owner or operator to provoke interpleader or concursus through which all claimants are required to litigate their claims against him in a single proceeding in federal court, without trial by jury. The vessel owner or operator may institute limitation proceedings without admitting liability to the claimants, i.e., the owner may institute the proceeding to seek exoneration or alternatively limitation. Ordinarily, he will provoke limitation but deny liability; if he is exonerated, he owes nothing, but if he is found at fault, he nevertheless may be able to limit his liability to the value of his vessel.

Limitation of liability was adopted by Congress before the corporate device developed into an effective method of doing business, before comprehensive insurance protection was generally available, and before modern forms of bankruptcy evolved. Limitation serves an analogous function to the corporate vehicle: encouraging investment of funds in a venture by permitting the investor to limit his personal financial responsibility to the amount which he has invested. With universal acceptance of the corporate device, the general availability of liability insurance, the adoption of other liability-limiting statutes such as the Carriage of Goods by the Sea Act, *see* Chapter IV, and the prevalence and relative ease of bankruptcy, the need for limitation as a means of encouraging investment in maritime commerce is questionable. Even if there is a need, the American limitation proceeding is nevertheless subject to criticism because it extends to situations which have little or no connection with maritime shipping and commerce, such as non-collision accidents aboard small pleasure craft.

Even if it has some value in the promotion of maritime shipping and commerce, limitation has developed in ways which make it an inequitable remedy. The operator of a vessel entitled to limitation need surrender only the vessel or its value after the occurrence; if, as is frequently the case, the vessel is sunk or heavily damaged, the limitation fund available to the claimants may be insignificant. In most states, a liability insurer is required to pay only the damages which the insured becomes legally obligated to pay to third persons; since limitation reduces the legal obligation of the insured, the beneficiary of the remedy usually is an insurer which has been compensated for underwriting the particular risk which has occurred. The vessel's owner or operator, however, fares better than the claimants his vessel has injured. His hull insurance does not form part of the limitation fund. *Place v. Norwich and N.Y. Transportation Co. (The City of Norwich)* (S.Ct.1886). The vessel owner may retain the proceeds of such insurance, although those damaged by his vessel recover little or nothing. It is not surprising, then, that limitation is unpopular. Gilmore & Black note that in modern (and postmodern) times "the limitation principle has been attacked by many and defended by almost none," and that calls for its repeal have "become a commonplace." Gilmore & Black, *supra,* at page 822.

While it remains, however, limitation plays an important role in allocation of damages resulting from maritime catastrophes and perhaps an even more important role in the tactics and strategies of maritime personal injury litigation. Limitation permits the owner to surrender the vessel and pending freight (or a sum equal to their value) and walk away from the debts of the voyage in which the accident occurred, or, if there is no voyage, from the debts arising out of the accident. The owner must surrender the vessel, or its value at the end of the voyage or after the accident, free of all liens arising prior to the voyage or accident. The 1976 Convention on Limitation of Liability for Maritime Claims bases the limitation fund upon the vessel's tonnage, and not its post-casualty value. However, that Convention, effective in 1986, has not been adopted by the United States.

In nearly all courts, the underlying contract or wrongful conduct which provokes the limitation policy will fall under admiralty jurisdiction. *See, e.g. Grubert, supra* at 39; *Sisson, supra* at 39. However, there is some authority for the proposition that the limitation statute provides an independent basis of federal jurisdiction. *See, e.g., In re Bernstein* (D. Mass. 1999); *see also*, Chapter XIX. The United States Supreme Court has left the question unanswered. *Grubert, supra* at 39; *Sisson, supra* at 39.

The owner and demise charterer, whether individual, partnership or corporation, may claim the benefits of the limitation statute. A part owner may limit his liability to an amount equal to the value of his share of the vessel. Limitation is available to the owners of "all seagoing vessels, and also to all vessels used on lakes or rivers or in inland navigation." 46 U.S.C.A. § 188. Thus the owner of a pleasure boat or of an 18–foot rowboat is entitled to limitation if the accident falls within admiralty jurisdiction. Since most pleasure boat accidents will have maritime "flavor," *see* Chapter III, pleasure boat owners (including jet ski owners) usually are entitled to limitation of liability if the accident occurs on navigable waters. *See, e.g., Matter of Guglielmo* (2d Cir.1990). The result has not escaped criticism and some judicial dissent. *See Matter of*

Lowing (W.D.Mich.1986), and the cases cited therein.

If two or more ships owned by the same person are involved in the incident for which limitation is sought, the owner in some instances may be required to surrender both vessels, and not merely the offending one. The "flotilla doctrine" requires the surrender of all vessels involved in performance of a contract when those vessels are subject to common ownership and are engaged in a single enterprise under a single command. *See, e.g., Valley Line Co. v. Ryan* (8th Cir.1985). The "pure tort" exception to the "flotilla rule" provides that if the injury is to a third person to whom the shipowner does not owe a duty based upon consent, he may limit his liability to the ship against which a maritime lien would arise from the wrong, as opposed to the value of the entire "flotilla." *See, e.g., In re Libel of Kristie Leigh* (5th Cir.1999).

Under the original American limitation statute, the limitation fund encompassed only the value of the vessel at the conclusion of the voyage. After a marine disaster in 1934 which claimed 135 lives, the vessel owner petitioned to limit his liability to the salvage value of his vessel, about $20,000. The resulting public outcry prompted Congress to enact legislation increasing the shipowner's responsibilities for vessel accidents causing death or personal injury. The most notable legislation was the so-called "Loss of Life Amendments," 46 U.S.C.A. § 183(b)–(f). These sections define a "seagoing vessel," and provide that if the owner of such a vessel is entitled to limitation and there are claims for personal injury or death, the limitation fund must provide a total minimum payment of $420.00 per ton (raised from $60 per ton by a 1984 amendment) to such claimants. For example, if limitation is sought and the vessel, after the occurrence, has a salvage value of only $20,000, but the vessel weighed 10,000 tons and there are personal injury and death claims, the limitation fund would be calculated in the following manner: (1) the personal injury and death claimants would receive their proportionate share of the distribution from the general limitation fund of $20,000; (2) if the amount received from that fund was insufficient to satisfy their claims, the personal injury and death claimants would be protected by an additional fund consisting of the difference between $4,200,000 ($420 per ton times 10,000 tons) and the total amount which they together received from the general limitation fund of $20,000.

The owner is liable for the $420 per ton fund on each "distinct occasion" in which loss of life or bodily injury occurs. 46 U.S.C.A. § 183(d). Although section 189 permits the owner of any "vessel" to limit liability, the Loss of Life Amendments apply only to owners of "seagoing vessels," the definition of which excludes pleasure yachts, tugs and towboats, fishing boats and other vessels usually not engaged in carrying passengers for hire. One court has defined a "seagoing vessel" as used in the Loss of Life Amendments as one that, considering its design, function, purpose and capabilities, may normally be expected to engage in substantial operations beyond the boundary line (set by the Coast Guard) dividing inland waters from the high seas. *Matter of Talbott Big Foot, Inc.*, (5th Cir.1988). The statutory and jurisprudential definitions would exclude most pleasure boats, creating the anomaly that a water venture which bears a minimum relationship to maritime shipping and commerce may be treated by admiralty law more favorably than oceangoing commercial vessels. Congress has amended the "Loss of Life Amendment" to add § 183(g), making state medical malpractice limitations on recovery applicable in certain maritime medical malpractice cases.

Ordinarily, the claimants in a maritime catastrophe will proceed against the shipowner and will not join his insurer, since the shipowner's liability policy will contain a "no action" clause barring suit against the insurer until judgment has been rendered against the insured. However, some states have adopted "direct action" statutes which nullify "no action" clauses and permit a claimant to institute suit against the insurer without first obtaining judgment against the insured. The issue of whether a "direct action" may be maintained against the vessel owner's liability insurer when the vessel owner has provoked limitation came before the Supreme Court in *Maryland Casualty Co. v. Cushing* (S.Ct.1954). Four members of the Court concluded that the "direct action" statute conflicted with limitation, and could not be applied. Their reasoning was that if the insurer's liability was exhausted through payment of judgments in "direct actions" prior to a determination of the limitation proceeding, the owner would be required to pay the limitation fund his insurer otherwise would have paid. This would mean that maintenance of a "direct action" would deny the owner the benefit of his insurance, violating the long-standing maritime policy that the owner in a limitation proceeding is entitled to the benefit of his insurance. *See The City of Norwich*, page 347, *supra,*. Four dissenters saw no conflict and would have permitted the claimant to maintain a "direct action." The ninth member of the Court, Justice Clark, proposed the solution that the "direct action" be stayed until determination of the limitation proceeding; if the policy limits were not exhausted by the limitation fund, or the matter was not mooted by exoneration of the vessel owner, the claimants then could continue the "direct action" for whatever insurer liability remained under the policy. Most of the subsequent cases have arisen in the U.S. Fifth Circuit, where intensive maritime activity and the Louisiana "direct action" statute coalesce. That court has instructed its lower courts to permit the "direct action," but to devise effective procedures, such as stay or consolidation, to assure that the owner is not deprived of the benefit of his insurance.

When the "direct action" is permitted, another issue arises: is the defense of limitation personal to the insured shipowner, or may it be urged by the insurer in a "direct action"? The Fifth Circuit initially held that the defense is personal to the insured. However, it later upheld, under the applicable state law, a policy provision which limited the underwriter's liability to the dollar amount for which the shipowner-assured was liable after it successfully maintained the right to limit liability. *Crown Zellerbach Corp. v. Ingram Indus., Inc.* (5th Cir.1986).

B. DEBTS INCURRED WITHOUT PRIVITY OR KNOWLEDGE

The vessel owner may only limit his liability for those debts which were incurred without his privity or knowledge. 46 U.S.C.A. § 183(a). As Gilmore & Black observe, the words "privity or knowledge" are "empty containers into which the courts are free to pour whatever content they will." Gilmore & Black, *supra,* page 877. Because of the harshness of the limitation remedy and the vagueness of the terms "privity or knowledge," it is not surprising that most limitation litigation has centered around whether there is "privity or knowledge." While the concept remains elusive, some general rules have evolved.

The initial inquiry is whether the claim for which limitation is sought sounds in tort or in contract. If the claim is in tort, "privity or knowledge" means the owner's personal participation in the negligence or fault which caused the damage. The negligence which constitutes privity, however, is not necessarily the same as some other forms of maritime negligence, such as in Jones Act claims. *See, e.g., Brister v. A.W.I., Inc.* (5th Cir.1991). If the owner is an individual, he usually fares well under the "privity or knowledge" test. He is not required to supervise his vessel, either at sea or in port. If he selects competent personnel and gives them adequate instructions, he will not be charged with "privity or knowledge" of their subsequent negligent acts. There are a number of exceptions to the rule, however. The first is that the individual owner of a "seagoing vessel" who seeks to limit liability for personal injury or death is charged with the "privity or knowledge" of the master of the vessel or of the owner's superintendent or managing agent at or prior to the commencement of each voyage. 46 U.S.C.A. § 183(e). The second is that if the individual owner delegates all management and control of his vessel to another, the delegate may become the owner's "alter ego" and the owner may be chargeable with the delegate's "privity or knowledge." Finally, the owner may be chargeable with "privity or knowledge" if he is in active control of the vessel at the time the claim arises. *See, e.g., Complaint of Ingoglia* (C.D. Cal.1989). If the owner is aboard the vessel but not in active control when the claim arises, he probably will be entitled to limitation only if he could not reasonably be expected to have discovered or prevented the negligent acts of his employees under the circumstances of the case.

If the shipowner is a corporation, application of the "privity or knowledge" exception is exceedingly difficult. As the Supreme Court has observed, "[a] corporation necessarily acts through human beings.

The privity of some of those persons must be the privity of the corporation else it could always limit its liability." *Coryell v. Phipps* (S.Ct.1943). There is, of course, the other side of the coin: if the "privity" of every corporate employee is "privity" of the corporation, then a negligent corporate shipowner could never limit its liability. The Act offers no aid in the solution of this problem; its drafters in the mid-nineteenth century understandably were thinking of shipowners as individuals, and not as corporations. Other than to rule that a corporation is entitled to limit its liability, the Supreme Court has provided little guidance.

Without help from higher authority, the lower courts have struggled with the problem. Generally speaking, courts will deny limitation of liability if the corporate fault which contributed to the damage was that of "high level managerial personnel," i.e., an officer or employee vested with discretion or authority with respect to the corporate activity which produced the damage. The employee's responsibilities, rather than his or her title, are critical. *In re Hellenic Inc.* (5th Cir.2001). This may, in some circumstances, include the master. *See, e.g., Potomac Transp., Inc. v. Ogden Marine, Inc.* (2d Cir.1990). Unlike the individual owner, the corporate owner may not escape liability for negligent conduct occurring in port by delegating a task to another; the corporate "high level managerial personnel" probably will be charged with whatever they could have discovered in the exercise of reasonable care in supervising the vessel's activities. A corporate owner which sends out an unseaworthy vessel may be denied limitation because "high level managerial personnel" failed to discover the condition prior to sailing or were negligent in their supervision of those persons charged with making the vessel seaworthy. If the claims involved in the limitation are personal injury or death claims, the corporate owner, like the individual owner, is chargeable with the "privity or knowledge" of the master, superintendent or managing agent at or prior to the commencement of each voyage, pursuant to the Loss of Life Amendments. 46 U.S.C.A. § 183(d)-(e).

In *Richardson v. Harmon* (S.Ct.1911), the Supreme Court ruled that an owner who is entitled to limitation nevertheless remains liable for "his own fault, neglect, *and contracts*." (emphasis added). This language led to the creation of the amorphous "personal contract" doctrine, i.e., the shipowner may not limit his liability for those contracts which are deemed "personal." A "personal contract," however, is not necessarily one which is executed personally by the owner. Charter parties are personal contracts but bills of lading are not, even though personally executed by the owner. Contracts for supplies or repairs which are entered into at the vessel's home port, and probably those entered into elsewhere, are personal contracts. There is authority for the proposition that the owner will be denied limitation under the "personal contract" doctrine only if the contract and the breach of the contract are both personal. *The Soerstad* (S.D.N.Y.1919). For example, although a contract to tow is "personal," the breach of the tower's duty to tow in a non-negligent manner may not be a "personal" one. The Limitation Act, 46 U.S.C.A. § 189, excludes seaman's wages from limitation, and it is arguable that maintenance and cure claims arise out of the owner's "personal contract" with the seaman and are not subject to limitation.

There are cases holding that claims for unearned prepaid freight and for damages to cargo through deviation of the voyage are not subject to limitation. Claims under the Wreck Act and the Rivers and Harbors Act (*See* Chapter XII) also are not limitable.

The final provision of the limitation statute is an enigma. In 1884 Congress added an additional section, now 46 U.S.C.A. § 189, which provides cryptically that "[t]he individual liability of a shipowner shall be limited to the proportion of any ... debts that his individual share of the vessel bears to the whole." Read literally, this later expression of Congressional intent could eliminate the "privity or knowledge" exception. It has not received such an interpretation, however, and generally has been ignored by the courts.

C. PROCEDURE IN LIMITATION OF LIABILITY

46 U.S.C.A. § 185 provides that

[t]he vessel owner, within six months after a claimant shall have given to ... such owner writ-

> ten notice of claim, may petition a district court
> . . . for limitation of liability within the provisions
> of this chapter.

This provision, added in 1936, is jurisdictional; thus
the right to limit liability through a concursus or
interpleader proceeding in federal admiralty court is
lost if the owner does not seek the relief within six
months after receipt of the first claim in writing
against him arising out of the occurrence. Supplemental Rule F(1), Admiralty and Maritime Claims,
28 U.S.C.A.; *Esta Later Charters, Inc. v. Ignacio*
(9th Cir.1989). The period may be extended if the
claims arise out of "distinct occasions." *Exxon Shipping Co. v. Cailleteau* (5th Cir.1989). The period
may not necessarily commence when the shipowner
receives notice of a claim against him; arguably, it
does not begin until he has notice that the claims
urged against him exceed the value of his vessel. A
letter setting forth key sufficient facts can constitute notice for purposes of commencing the six-
month period. *Paradise Divers, Inc. v. Upmal* (11th
Cir.2005).

It seems clear that the vessel owner does *not* lose
the right to seek limitation as an affirmative defense if he fails to provoke the concursus proceeding
within the six-month period. There are cases up-
holding the use of limitation as a defense in an
action in federal court after the six-month period
has expired, *but* there is some dicta, including some
from the Supreme Court, to the contrary. The cases
and the dicta, in *M/S Bremen v. Zapata Off–Shore*

Co., page 130, *supra*, are discussed in Gilmore & Black, *supra*, pages 855–57.

If the vessel owner who has failed to seek limitation in admiralty within the six-month period is sued in state court, he encounters the additional argument that a state court may lack jurisdiction to apply limitation, even as a defense. *See, e.g., Vatican Shrimp Co., Inc. v. Solis* (5th Cir.1987). However, the better view is that limitation should be available as a defense in either state or federal court. *Karim v. Finch Shipping Co., Ltd.* (5th Cir. 2001). There is of course another danger to the shipowner who permits the six-month period to elapse without commencing a limitation concursus proceeding; even if he is permitted to urge limitation as a defense in separate suits, he may be required to make separate deposits of the total amount of the limitation fund in each of the suits. *Signal Oil & Gas Co. v. Barge W–701* (5th Cir. 1981).

The limitation concursus proceeding is governed by 46 U.S.C.A. § 185, Supplemental Rule F, Admiralty and Maritime Claims, and by local court rules. The shipowner provoking limitation must surrender title to the vessel, or file a bond in the amount of the value of the vessel. The posting of the bond probably is not jurisdictional and thus the failure to file it within the six month period is not fatal. *See, e.g., Guey v. Gulf Ins. Co.* (5th Cir.1995). When a petition for limitation is filed, the court enjoins the commencement or continuation elsewhere of claims arising out of the voyage or event for which limitation is sought, and fixes a time for the filing of claims in the limitation proceeding. Notice is given to the known claimants and is published. Claimants must file their answers and claims within the designated delay. When that delay has expired, each claimant who has filed a claim is notified of the other claims which have been filed, and the matter proceeds to trial in the normal course of litigation. The delay for filing claims is not jurisdictional; the court may excuse a late filing. The party provoking the limitation and the claimants may file counterclaims and cross claims against each other, so that all of the claims arising out of the maritime disaster may be litigated in one proceeding. *British Transp. Comm'n v. United States (The Haiti Victory)* (S.Ct. 1957).

In most cases, the vessel owner will deny liability, and will urge his right to limitation in the alternative. When this occurs, the claimants initially bear the burden of establishing the vessel owner's liability. If they fail to do so, the owner is exonerated, and the limitation proceeding is mooted. If the claimants are successful in establishing liability, the burden shifts to the owner to prove that the liability was incurred without his "privity or knowledge" and that he is otherwise entitled to limit his liability to the value of his vessel. *See, e.g., Suzuki of Orange Park, Inc. v. Shubert* (11th Cir.1996).

Since jurisdiction over a limitation proceeding is within the exclusive jurisdiction of the admiralty "side" of federal court, limitation issues are not triable to a jury. Thus limitation conflicts with the maritime policy of granting a claimant the option of trial by jury, a policy espoused by Congress (the "saving to suitors" clause) and by the judiciary. *Romero v. International Terminal Operating Co.*, page 5, *supra* and *Fitzgerald v. United States Lines Co.* (S.Ct.1963). *See also* Chapter XIX. What has emerged in the jurisprudence is an accommodation in which a claimant is permitted to obtain jury trial (as a law claim in federal court, or in state court) on the issues of liability and damages if such a trial would not undermine the protection to which the shipowner is entitled under limitation. Thus a claimant may obtain a modification of the injunction against "other proceedings" provided by Supplemental Rule F(3) so that he may prosecute his claim in state court or at law in federal court if (1) his claim is the only claim against the vessel owner, *Ex parte Green* (S.Ct.1932), *Langnes v. Green* (S.Ct. 1931), or (2) the total amount of all claims does not exceed the limitation fund. *Lake Tankers Corp. v. Henn* (S.Ct.1957). In such cases, one of the reasons for the concursus or interpleader in limitation is absent: either there is no exposure of the shipowner to liability beyond the value of his vessel, or no possibility of duplicative or conflicting fact finding on the issues of liability and damages. In either case, however, the litigants must return to federal court for determination of the limitation issues, if those issues are not mooted by the disposition made in the other court.

Since injunctive relief ordinarily is discretionary, it is arguable that a judge may lift the injunction

and permit litigation in state court whenever equitable considerations justify such action. Some jurisprudence suggests that the judge may modify the
injunction and permit litigation in state court only
if the "single claim" or "adequate fund" criteria
described above are present. However, courts generally are liberal in finding a "single claim," *see, e.g.,
Complaint of Midland Enterprises, Inc.* (6th Cir.
1989), and in lifting the injunction when the claimant makes stipulations that eliminate any prejudice
to the limitation defense by allowing the matter to
proceed first in another court. The stipulations are
becoming uniform and complex. *See, e.g., Texaco,
Inc. v. Williams* (5th Cir.1995)*; Complaint of Dam-
mers & Vanderheide* (2d Cir.1988). Defendants had
sometimes argued that in order to be allowed to
proceed in state court a claimant had to stipulate
that the federal court had exclusive jurisdiction over
both exoneration and limitation. The United States
Supreme Court implicitly rejected that argument in
Lewis v. Lewis & Clark Marine, Inc. (S.Ct.2001).
The Fifth Circuit expressly did so in *In re Tetra
Applied Technologies, L.P.*, (5th Cir.2004).

Supplemental Admiralty Rule F(8) provides that
"the fund ... shall be divided pro rata, subject to
all relevant provisions of law, among the several
claimants in proportion to the amounts of their
respective claims ... saving, however, to all parties
any priority to which they may be legally entitled."
The uncertainty of lien rankings, *see* page 108 *supra*, thus carries over into the distribution of the
limitation fund. Some courts have used equitable

principles in distributing an inadequate limitation fund.

D. CHOICE OF LAW IN LIMITATION PROCEEDINGS

While limitation is a generally accepted principle of maritime law, there are no uniform international rules. Many nations adhere to the 1957 Brussels Convention rules, while the United States and Great Britain each has its own limitation scheme, with differing methods of calculating the limitation fund. For example, American law is more favorable to the death or personal injury claimant than British law.

Since 46 U.S.C.A. § 183 makes American limitation law applicable to foreign vessels, a foreign shipowner may seek limitation in an American admiralty court; when this occurs, the question of choice of limitation law arises. As a general proposition, the American courts treat limitation as procedural rather than substantive, and apply the law of the forum, i.e., the American law. There is at least one qualification, however. Congress has prescribed the application of foreign limitation law in some wrongful death actions. 46 U.S.C.A. § 764 provides:

> Whenever a right of action is granted by the law of any foreign State on account of death by wrongful act ... occurring upon the high seas, such right may be maintained in an appropriate action in admiralty in the courts of the United States without abatement in respect to the

amount for which recovery is authorized, any statute of the United States to the contrary notwithstanding.

Thus under certain circumstances if the death is caused by injury occurring outside American territorial waters, the American limitation act may not be applied to reduce recovery.

The "substance-procedure" rule arose out of the decision of the United States Supreme Court in *Oceanic Steam Navigation Co. v. Mellor (The Titanic)* (S.Ct.1914). At that time the "substance-procedure" distinction was of great significance in the choice of laws. Its application nearly a century later to make a choice of the law that determines the amount of damage a tortfeasor must pay seems incongruous. The matter would best be resolved under modern choice of law principles, and in fact nearly all the decisions since *The Titanic* are consistent with the application of those principles. Under such principles, the court should evaluate the interests of the forum state and other sovereigns in applying their limitation law to the claims involved. If limitation is sought in an American court, and the vessel is American owned or operated or the accident occurred in American waters, American limitation law ordinarily should be applied. If the accident occurs on the high seas, a federal court should apply American law as the law of the forum, unless there is some other sovereign with an overriding interest in the outcome of the litigation, such as where the vessel and claimants are of the same nationality. If the accident occurs within the territorial waters of another sovereign, that sovereign's law ordinarily should apply, particularly if that sovereign treats limitation as part of its substantive law. *See, e.g., Karim v. Finch Shipping Co., Ltd., I & II* (5th Cir.2004 and 2001); *In re Korea Shipping Corp., Ltd.* (9th Cir.1990).

CHAPTER XIX

JURISDICTION AND PRO-
CEDURE IN MARI-
TIME CLAIMS

A. HISTORY

Prior to the American Revolution, English law developed three court systems—law, equity and admiralty—which exercised jurisdiction over different types of controversies. The admiralty court was the outgrowth of the informal "port courts" which initially resolved maritime disputes. The concept of separate courts of law, equity and admiralty was imported into the colonies, and subsequently survived the Revolution and the adoption of the Constitution. In the early days of the federal judiciary, however, a single judge performed all three functions in a given geographical area; as a result, each federal court had three dockets or "sides"—law, equity and admiralty. If a matter was brought before the court and jurisdiction was based upon the federal admiralty power, the case would be placed on the admiralty docket and would be processed through application of special admiralty rules by a judge "sitting in admiralty" and lawyers sometimes called "proctors in admiralty."

The first major change came in 1938, when the Federal Rules of Civil Procedure were adopted and made applicable in all cases of law and equity. This produced a unification of the law and equity "sides" of federal court, but admiralty remained separate, and the special admiralty rules continued to govern cases on the admiralty "side." In 1966, the Federal Rules were made applicable to cases in which the federal court is exercising jurisdiction through the admiralty power. This seemingly sounded the death knell for the admiralty "side" of the federal court, but, to borrow a phrase, the news of its death was greatly exaggerated. The 1966 effort at unification made nearly all of the Federal Rules of Civil Procedure applicable in admiralty matters, but the rulemakers retained a number of special rules which apply only when the federal court is exercising jurisdiction through the admiralty power. For example, amended Rule 38(e) provides that "[t]hese rules shall not be construed to create a right to trial by jury of the issues in an admiralty or maritime claim," and amended Rule 14(c) continues, in maritime claims, a unique admiralty third party practice. The merged rules do not affect venue; thus the special admiralty venue rules continue in maritime matters. Finally, special supplemental rules for certain maritime matters were adopted as an appendix to the general rules. Thus despite the 1966 "unification," significant procedural differences still exist if the jurisdiction of the federal court is premised upon the admiralty power. Accordingly, it still is appropriate to speak, in a limited sense, about the admiralty "side" of federal court and the term continues as a shorthand way of referring to a case pending in federal court in which jurisdiction is based upon the federal admiralty power, *i.e.*, when it is brought as an admiralty claim. In the remainder of this chapter, we explore the situations in which a matter may or must be brought as an admiralty claim in federal court, and discuss some of the procedural issues that arise out of the selection of a forum.

B.   SUBJECT MATTER JURISDICTION

If a claim falls within the federal admiralty power, Congress can prescribe which courts may adjudicate it. *See* Chapter I, *supra*. Congress made the primary allocation of subject matter jurisdiction over matters "in admiralty" in section 9 of the Judiciary Act of 1789, now 28 U.S.C.A. § 1333, which provides:

The district courts shall have original jurisdiction, exclusive of the courts of the States, of:

(1) Any civil case of admiralty or maritime jurisdiction, saving to suitors in all cases all other remedies to which they are otherwise entitled. . . .

Thus if a matter falls within the federal admiralty power, a federal district court has subject matter jurisdiction by virtue of section 1333. If the court's only basis of jurisdiction is section 1333, the case properly may be said to be on what remains of the admiralty "side" of federal court after the attempted unification in 1966. The primary feature of this admiralty "side" is that there is no constitutional or statutory right to trial by jury.

The "saving to suitors" clause in 28 U.S.C.A. § 1333 initially provided that what was "saved" was "the right of a common law remedy, where the common law is competent to give it." Section 9, Judiciary Act of 1789, 1 Stats. 76, 77. For over a century, argument raged over whether what was "saved" was the common law cause of action, or the right to proceed in common law courts to enforce the maritime cause of action. It now is settled that what is "saved" is the right to enforce the maritime cause of action in a law court, which may be either the state court or a federal court that has jurisdiction at law by virtue of diversity of citizenship or the existence of an independent federal question. *See* Chapter I. Thus if a matter is "in admiralty," maritime substantive law applies, regardless of the court in which it is heard.

It also is settled that the common law "is competent to give" all maritime remedies except *in rem* proceedings. The term "*in rem* proceeding" is used here in the strict and not the broader sense. The distinction, as pointed out in *Pennoyer v. Neff* (S.Ct. 1877), is that:

> In a strict sense, a proceeding *in rem* is one taken directly against property, and has for its object the disposition of property, without reference to the title of individual claimants; but, in a larger and more general sense, the terms are applied to

actions between parties, where the direct object is to reach and dispose of property owned by them, or some interest therein. Such are cases commenced by attachment against the property of debtors, or instituted to partition real estate, foreclose a mortgage, or enforce a lien.... They are substantially proceedings *in rem* in the broader sense.

Maritime law authorizes the use of the *in rem* proceeding—in the strict sense—to enforce a maritime lien or a preferred mortgage against a vessel; the vessel is made the defendant, and a judicial sale in the proceeding conveys title "good against the world." Section 1333, then, conveys exclusive jurisdiction to the federal court, sitting in admiralty, over all proceedings *in rem* to enforce a maritime lien or preferred ship mortgage. All other maritime matters are those in which "the common law is competent to give" a remedy and therefore may be brought in state court, unless Congress by some other statute has vested exclusive jurisdiction in federal courts or a federal administrative agency.

There is one notable exception to the rule that all maritime *in rem* proceedings must be brought as admiralty claims in federal court. In *C.J. Hendry Co. v. Moore* (S.Ct.1943), the Supreme Court upheld a state forfeiture proceeding (the functional equivalent of an *in rem* proceeding in the strict sense) in state court against a net which had been used for fishing in navigable waters in violation of state law. The Court reached this conclusion after determining that common law courts historically exercised jurisdiction *in rem* in the enforcement of forfeiture statutes, concurrently with the courts of admiralty; thus, this was an *in rem* remedy which "the common law is competent to give."

The admiralty "side" of federal court has exclusive jurisdiction over limitation of liability concursus proceedings, 46 U.S.C.A. § 185, *see* Chapter XVIII, and suits against the sovereign, either under the Suits in Admiralty Act, 46 U.S.C.A. § 741 et seq., *see* Chapter XVI, or under the Public Vessels Act, 46 U.S.C.A. § 781 et seq., *see* Chapter XVI. There is strong dicta in *Offshore Logistics, Inc. v. Tallentire*, page 311, *supra*, that jurisdiction over DOHSA claims is concurrent between the federal court sitting in admiralty and state court. Jurisdiction over Jones Act claims, 46 U.S.C.A. § 688, is concurrent between federal and state courts.

If a federal law is enacted which regulates substantive admiralty rights but does not make an express grant of subject matter jurisdiction, the case may be brought in federal court, either as an admiralty claim under 28 U.S.C.A. § 1333 ("civil case of admiralty or maritime jurisdiction") or at law, under 28 U.S.C.A. § 1331, (it "arises under" a federal statute), or in state court (under the "savings to suitors" clause of section 1333).

A general maritime law claim (within the admiralty power but not arising out of a federal statute) may be brought as an admiralty claim under 28 U.S.C.A. § 1333, and, unless the litigant seeks enforcement of a claim *in rem*, it also may be brought

in state court under the "savings to suitors" clause.
It may not be brought as a law claim in federal
court unless there is diversity jurisdiction (complete
diversity of citizenship and an amount in controver-
sy exceeding $75,000). 28 U.S.C.A. § 1332. The
Supreme Court has rejected the contention that a
maritime common law claim may be brought in
federal court as a law claim because it "arises
under" the Constitution (Art. III, Sec. 2, cl. 3).
Although the federal power to prescribe general
maritime law stems from the Constitution, a general maritime law remedy does not "arise under" the
constitution within the meaning of the statute conveying "federal question" jurisdiction, 28 U.S.C.A.
§ 1331. *Romero v. International Terminal Co.*, page
5, *supra*. Examples of these kinds of claims which
may not be brought as law claims in federal court
unless there is diversity jurisdiction are general
maritime tort and contract claims and the seaman's
remedies of maintenance and cure and unseaworthiness.

The most important distinction between the law
and admiralty "sides" of federal court is that trial
by jury is guaranteed for law claims through the
Seventh Amendment, but if the case is maintained
as an admiralty claim, the litigant has neither constitutional nor statutory right to a jury trial. The
one exception is the "Great Lakes rule," a special
statute providing

> In any case of admiralty and maritime jurisdic-
> tion relating to any matter of contract or tort
> arising upon or concerning any vessel of twenty

tons or upward, enrolled and licensed for the coasting trade, and employed in the business of commerce and navigation between places in different states upon the lakes and navigable waters connecting said lakes, the trial of all issues of fact shall be by jury if either demands it.

28 U.S.C.A. § 1873. With this exception, a litigant may not demand trial by jury in federal court if jurisdiction is premised solely upon the admiralty power.

Litigation of a matter as an admiralty claim in federal court frequently provides a judge who is skilled in and sympathetic to maritime concerns, but, except when 28 U.S.C.A. § 1873 applies, it does not provide trial by jury. When a maritime matter is brought in state court, there may be trial by jury (depending upon state law), but the state judge is not likely to be as attuned to federal admiralty concerns, or as conversant with the intricacies of maritime law, as his federal counterpart. Understandably, a maritime litigant may want to present his maritime common law claim to a jury in federal court. There is one important way in which that goal may be attained. While a litigant in federal court whose claim is premised solely upon admiralty common law may not demand trial by jury, there is no constitutional or statutory bar to a jury trial of such a claim. If the maritime claim is the only claim before the court, trial by jury is inappropriate; the federal policy generally favoring jury trials is counterbalanced by the goal of judicial efficiency, since granting trial by jury in such a case would burden the federal judiciary with an otherwise unnecessary jury trial. But what if a matter which is cognizable at law is properly joined with a matter brought as an admiralty claim and the litigant seeks trial by jury on the law claim? The trial may be bifurcated, with the judge sitting as trier of fact in the maritime claim. However, if the claims are properly joined, they ordinarily will arise out of the same factual situation, and permitting a jury trial on both claims will not burden the federal judiciary with an additional jury trial on those facts. Thus the federal policy favoring jury trials can be served without a corresponding disservice to the goal of judicial economy. Accordingly, the Supreme Court has ruled that if a "federal question" claim is properly joined with a maritime claim brought on the admiralty "side," and both "grow out of a single transaction or accident," the litigant may obtain trial by jury of both matters. *Fitzgerald v. United States Lines Co.*, page 218 *supra*. One typical case is joinder of a Jones Act negligence action, for which trial by jury is statutorily provided, with claims for unseaworthiness and maintenance and cure. If there is diversity jurisdiction over the unseaworthiness and maintenance and cure claims, and they are brought at law, the parties are entitled to trial by jury. If there is no diversity jurisdiction over them, the two claims can be brought in federal court only as admiralty claims. However, under Fed.Civ.Proc. Rules 18 or 20, the unseaworthiness and maintenance and cure claims may be joined with the Jones Act claim, which can be brought at law under 28 U.S.C.A.

§ 1331, and thus a litigant may have jury trial on all three claims. If the Jones Act claim which provides the trial by jury is dismissed prior to trial, the litigant probably will lose his right to jury trial on the appended maritime claims. If the Jones Act claim is dismissed during trial, the judge has discretion to submit the remaining claims to the jury.

The result may be different if the jurisdiction at law is based upon diversity of citizenship. If all of the defendants, including those against whom admiralty claims are asserted, are of diverse citizenship from the plaintiff, there is complete diversity and all of the matters may be tried to a jury if a party so elects. But if one of the admiralty claim defendants is not of diverse citizenship from the plaintiff, then, arguably the complete diversity required by *Strawbridge v. Curtiss* (S.Ct.1806), is lacking, and the court is without subject matter jurisdiction at law over the nonmaritime claims. Thus *Fitzgerald* should not apply because there is no "law" claim entitled to jury trial to which the "admiralty" claim can be pended. The counterargument, of course, is that what has occurred is merely a joinder of a maritime claim with a nonmaritime claim, and that since complete diversity exists over the nonmaritime claim, both claims may be tried to a jury under the *Fitzgerald* doctrine. *Compare Powell v. Offshore Navigation, Inc.* (5th Cir.1981), *with Vodusek v. Bayliner Marine Corp.* (4th Cir.1995).

Some actions may be brought in federal court either as admiralty claims or as law claims. One example is a Jones Act claim; another is an unseaworthiness or maintenance and cure claim in which there is diversity of citizenship and the requisite jurisdictional amount. In such cases, Fed.Civ.Proc. Rule 9(h), provides that the claim will be processed as a law claim unless the pleading setting forth the claim contains "a statement identifying the claim as an admiralty or maritime claim for the purposes of Rules 14(c), 38(e), 82, and the Supplemental Rules for Certain Admiralty and Maritime Claims."

C. JURISDICTION OVER THE PERSON

In a maritime *in rem* action, jurisdiction over the person of the "defendant," the vessel, is premised upon the presence of the vessel within the district in which the court sits. Jurisdiction usually is perfected by seizure of the vessel. Seizure, however, may not be essential to jurisdiction; the courts have upheld *in rem* jurisdiction if the vessel owner takes some action which fairly may be construed as a waiver of the lack of jurisdiction over the vessel, such as a "letter of undertaking" by which the owner agrees that the claimant's rights are the same as if the vessel had been seized and subsequently released by the filing of a claim and a release bond. *See, e.g., Panaconti Shipping Co., S.A. v. M/V Ypapanti* (5th Cir.1989). After jurisdiction *in rem* has attached, it generally is not lost if the res is removed from the control of the seizing court. *See, e.g., Republic National Bank v. United States* (S.Ct. 1992).

When a maritime matter is brought in state court or on the "law side" of federal court, the general rules governing jurisdiction over the person in those courts apply. The rules applicable to proceedings brought at law in federal court also govern jurisdiction over an *in personam* action brought as an admiralty claim, since there are no special statutes or rules governing jurisdiction over the person in maritime matters. A defendant may be compelled to litigate in a federal court if (1) he is "amenable," i.e., "the exercise of jurisdiction is consistent with the Constitution and laws of the United States," and (2) he may be served with process by the court asserting jurisdiction. In many instances the nonresident shipowner or other admiralty defendant will have sufficient contacts to satisfy the requirement of amenability and the issue of jurisdiction will turn upon whether service may be effected upon him within the district. The more important rules governing service upon nonresident shipowners are Rule 4(e), providing for personal or domiciliary service upon a defendant within the district or through use of the state's "long arm" statute, Rule 4(f), providing methods for service upon individuals in foreign countries, Rule 4(h), providing for service in the district upon a corporation or partnership by delivering a copy of the complaint to "an officer, a managing or general agent, or to any other agent authorized by appointment or by law to receive service of process," and Rule 4(k)(2), providing for service of process and personal jurisdiction in any district court for cases arising under federal law where the defendant has minimum contacts with the United States as a whole sufficient to satisfy due process concerns, but defendant is not subject to jurisdiction in any particular state.

A forum selection clause may confer personal jurisdiction over a party in some circumstances. A federal court sitting in admiralty also may assert a kind of *quasi in rem* jurisdiction over a nonresident through attachment, a traditional maritime remedy which has been continued in Supplemental Rules B and E, Admiralty and Maritime Claims. Under those rules attachment is proper if the defendant is not "found within the district." Supp. Rule B(1), Admiralty and Maritime Claims. "Found," in this context, means that the defendant is both subject to the jurisdiction of the court *and* can be served within the district. *See, e.g., LaBanca v. Ostermunchner* (5th Cir.1981). If the defendant has not engaged in sufficient activity in the district to make him amenable to suit there under due process and the applicable state or federal statutes exerting jurisdiction over the person, he can not be "found" in the district in the jurisdictional sense, and attachment is proper. Even if the defendant is amenable to suit *in personam* and thus is "found" within the district in the geographical sense, nonresident attachment may be effected if he may not be "found" for service of process, *i.e.,* if service may not be effected upon him within the district in the manner provided by Rule 4. Since "nonresidency" for attachment in admiralty is nonresidency within the district and not within the state, a claimant may attach property within a district in which the defendant cannot be served, although the defendant is amenable to service in, and can be served elsewhere in the state. This permits the claimant to use nonresident attachment as a means of obtaining security for the judgment which subsequently is rendered. That result has been subject to some criticism, but apparently was a deliberate choice of the rulemakers. See notes of advisory committee, Supp. Rule B, Admiralty and Maritime Claims. Supplemental Rule B also permits a plaintiff to utilize in admiralty court the attachment procedures provided by the state in which the court sits. Use of *quasi in rem* jurisdiction may permit a marine supplier to enforce his claim against a "sister ship" of the vessel he supplied.

When a defendant whose property has been seized in an *in rem* or *quasi in rem* action gives security for the plaintiff's claim and asserts a counterclaim "arising out of the same transaction or occurrence," the court has the power to order the plaintiff to "give security in the usual amount and form to respond in damages to the claims set forth in such counterclaim." Supplemental Rule E(7), Admiralty and Maritime Claims. When the court exercises its discretion to require such security, the proceedings on the original claim are stayed until the security is given. *See, e.g., Chan v. Society Expeditions, Inc.* (9th Cir.1994). Under 28 U.S.C. Sec. 2464(B) and Supplemental Rule E(5)(b), the court may require "further security" at any time; however, that may be limited to replacement security, and not an increase in the amount of security originally fixed by the court. *Moore v. M/V* Angela (5th Cir.2003).

Since the admiralty *in rem* and *quasi in rem* actions are devices by which jurisdiction is asserted through prejudgment seizure of property, the constitutionality of each has been challenged, under the due process "amenability" requirements of *Shaffer v. Heitner* (S.Ct.1977), and the due process "fair notice" rules laid down in *Fuentes v. Shevin* (S.Ct.1972), and its progeny. Under *Shaffer*, prejudgment seizure may not be used to effect jurisdiction unless there is a sufficient relationship among the forum state, the property and its presence in the state, the defendant, and the claim to make it reasonable for the forum state to exercise jurisdiction through seizure of the property. The *in rem* action frequently meets the *Shaffer* test, since the claim enforced in an *in rem* proceeding, the maritime lien, usually will have a close connection with the property and the "defendant," *i.e.*, the property itself. Nonresident attachment appears more constitutionally vulnerable, since there is no requirement of a relationship between the property attached and the claim sought to be enforced.

The *Fuentes* doctrine generally condemns prejudgment seizure unless there is a special need for prompt action, and the person initiating the seizure is a government official responsible for determining under standards of a narrowly drawn statute that the particular seizure is justified. Supplemental Rules B, C and E, Admiralty and Maritime Claims, initially did not require pre-seizure judicial supervision, making the maritime *in rem* and *quasi in rem* procedures suspect under *Fuentes*. Most admiralty courts determined that the admiralty pre-judgment seizures passed constitutional muster because the international and mobile character of vessels satisfied the *Fuentes* requirement of a need for prompt seizure, and because a speedy post-seizure hearing was available, either through a Rule 12 motion or local court rules. Concern for constitutionality, however, led to 1985 amendments to Supplemental Rules B and C. The amended rules require judicial scrutiny before the issuance of attachment, garnishment or a warrant of arrest of a vessel, unless "exigent circumstances make [pre-seizure] review by the court impracticable." Process may issue by the clerk if the plaintiff or his attorney certifies that "exigent circumstances" exist; in such a case, the vessel owner is entitled to a post-seizure hearing, Rule E(4)(f), at which the plaintiff has the burden of establishing that exigent circumstances did exist.

Service of process in an in rem proceeding must be made "forthwith," Rule E(4)(a); however, untimely but accomplished service may not defeat the court's jurisdiction. *United States v. 2,164 Watches, More or Less, Bearing Registered Trademark of Guess?, Inc.* (9th Cir.2004).

D. VENUE

There is no general venue requirement for an action brought as an admiralty claim in federal court; if the court has jurisdiction over the person, venue is proper. However, some maritime actions brought in federal court under the admiralty jurisdiction are subject to special venue rules; examples include proceedings for limitation of liability, Supplemental Rule F(9), Admiralty and Maritime Claims, and suits against the United States, 46 U.S.C.A. §§ 742, 782.

The provision in the Jones Act, 46 U.S.C.A. § 688(a) that "[j]urisdiction ... shall be under the court of the district in which the defendant employer resides or in which his principal office is located" has been interpreted as prescribing venue, and not jurisdiction. *Panama Railroad Co. v. Johnson* (S.Ct. 1924). Despite this venue provision, if the Jones Act case is brought as an admiralty claim the plaintiff may avail himself of the admiralty rule that venue is proper wherever jurisdiction over the person can be obtained.

When the Jones Act was adopted, its venue provision was broader than the general provision for venue in suits brought at law in federal court against corporations. However, the general venue provision, now 28 U.S.C.A. § 1391(c), was amended in 1948 to permit a corporation to be sued "in any judicial district in which it is incorporated or licensed to do business or is doing business." The Supreme Court has ruled that a claimant pursuing a Jones Act claim at law may avail himself of the now broader provisions of 28 U.S.C.A. § 1391(c), and is not restricted to the venue provided in the Jones Act. *Pure Oil Co. v. Suarez* (S.Ct.1966). A subsequent amendment to 28 U.S.C.A. § 1391 has further liberalized the venue rules for civil actions in which jurisdiction is not founded solely upon diversity, and those rules also should apply to Jones Act claims.

Statutes permitting transfer to a proper, 28 U.S.C.A. § 1406, or more convenient, 28 U.S.C.A. § 1404(a), forum apply in actions brought as admiralty claims in federal court. *Continental Grain Co. v. The FBL–585* (S.Ct.1960). Transfer to a more convenient forum merely moves the claim to another federal court. It must be distinguished from *forum non conveniens*, in which an action is dismissed and the parties are required to pursue the matter in the courts of another sovereign. The federal *forum non conveniens* rule, *see* Chapter XIII, *supra,* is not binding on a state court in a maritime matter. *American Dredging Co. v. Miller* (S.Ct. 1994).

E.   PROCEDURE IN MARITIME CLAIMS

When a maritime claim is brought in state court or at law in federal court, the applicable procedure is that used in processing other claims in the same courts, with one important exception: if there is an admiralty procedural rule which is an integral part of the substantive maritime right, that rule must be applied when the claim is processed in other courts. This principle is illustrated by *Garrett v. Moore–McCormack Co.* (S.Ct.1942), in which a seaman who had executed a release of his maritime claims subsequently brought an action on the claims in Pennsylvania state court. The maritime rule is that a party relying upon a seaman's release has the burden of proving the validity of the release, but Pennsylvania law placed the burden of proving the invalidity of the release upon the claimant who executed it. The Supreme Court held that the Pennsylvania courts erred in applying the state rule, noting:

> The right of the petitioner to be free from the burden of proof [of the invalidity of the release] imposed by the Pennsylvania local rule inhered in his cause of action. Deeply rooted in admiralty as that right is, *it was a part of the very substance of his claim and cannot be considered a mere incident of a form of procedure....* Pennsylvania having opened its courts to petitioner to enforce federally created rights, the petitioner was entitled to the full scope of those rights. (Emphasis added).

This is the converse of the rule, pronounced in *Byrd v. Blue Ridge Rural Electric Cooperative, Inc.* (S.Ct. 1958), that a federal court sitting in diversity must apply state procedural law which is an integral part of the state cause of action. There are few illustrations of the application of the *Garrett* rule in maritime law. The most common one is that if a Jones Act claim is brought in state court, the plaintiff's "featherweight" burden of proving causation applies, rather than a more stringent state court rule. One important issue is whether the non-availability of trial by jury in certain circumstances is an integral part of the maritime remedy. If a Jones Act claim is brought in state court, the seaman has a right to trial by jury without regard to state law. However, if there is an absence of diversity or federal question jurisdiction, a suit on any other maritime claim brought in federal court must be brought as an admiralty claim, and there is no trial by jury. Some litigants have argued that if the same claim is brought in state court the parties should not be entitled to trial by jury, even though jury trial otherwise would be available under state law, because trial to a judge alone is an integral part of the federal maritime right. This argument has been rejected by a state supreme court. *Lavergne v. Western Co. of North America, Inc.* (La.1979).

When a maritime claim is brought in federal court and jurisdiction is premised upon the admiralty power, the Federal Rules of Civil Procedure apply, with several important exceptions. One of these exceptions, the lack of jury trial, previously has been discussed. Another exception is that the Supplemental Rules for Certain Admiralty and Maritime Claims apply in *in rem* and *quasi in rem* actions, in possessory, petitory and partition actions, and in actions for exoneration from or limitation of liability. A third exception is that when the federal court's jurisdiction is based upon the admiralty power, a special third party practice is available under the provisions of Fed.Civ.Proc. Rule 14(c). The original federal third party rule, now Rule 14(a), permits a defendant to call in a third party who may be liable to the defendant in indemnity or contribution. Under Rule 14(a) a defendant may "pass on" to the third party all or part of defendant's liability to plaintiff, but plaintiff may not recover judgment directly against the third party unless he amends his complaint to assert a claim against the third party. Former Admiralty Rule 56 permitted the defendant to use third party practice to "pass on" his liability, but also permitted the defendant to assert the plaintiff's claim directly against the third party defendant, thus making the third party an "additional defendant" subject to judgment in favor of the plaintiff without any further pleadings on the part of the plaintiff. Fed.Civ. Proc. Rule 14(c), adopted as part of the unification in 1966, makes this "additional defendant" procedure available if the federal court is sitting in admiralty.

If jurisdiction over a claim brought in federal court may be sustained both under the admiralty power and under some other basis of jurisdiction, the matter is at law unless the plaintiff makes the declaration contemplated by Fed.Civ.Proc. Rule, 9(h), identifying the claim as an admiralty or maritime claim. A court may permit a plaintiff to amend his complaint to add or delete the Rule 9(h) declaration and transfer the case into or out of the admiralty docket, at least where jurisdiction at law is premised solely upon the Jones Act, and the defendant is not entitled to jury trial in his own right. *See, e.g., Rachal v. Ingram Corp.* (5th Cir.1986).

It is not clear whether a plaintiff may provoke an *in rem* proceeding and obtain a jury trial on a joined personal injury claim to which trial by jury ordinarily would be available. *See, e.g., Haskins v. Point Towing Co.* (3d Cir.1968).

F. REMOVAL

The general provision for removal of civil actions from state to federal court, 28 U.S.C.A. § 1441, applies to maritime actions commenced in state court, but not all such actions may be removed. Section 1441(a) provides:

> Except as otherwise expressly provided by Act of Congress, any civil action brought in a State court of which the district courts of the United States have original jurisdiction, may be removed....

Congress has expressly provided, in 28 U.S.C.A. § 1445, that a FELA claim commenced in state court is not removable; the adoption of the FELA by the Jones Act has been interpreted to include this prohibition against removal. Accordingly, a Jones Act claim commenced in state court is not removable, even if there is federal jurisdiction independent of the Jones Act, such as diversity jurisdiction.

The traditional rule was that if the state court did not have subject matter jurisdiction, the matter could not be removed. Thus if a maritime *in rem* action was brought in state court, the appropriate remedy was dismissal. A 1986 statute, now 28 U.S.C.A. § 1441(e), now permits removal of *in rem* cases brought in state court.

Other maritime cases commenced in state court ordinarily may be removed to the law "side" of federal court, if the requisites for diversity jurisdiction are present or if there is "federal question" jurisdiction. However, a maritime common law claim does not fall within the court's "federal question" jurisdiction under 28 U.S.C.A. § 1331, although it "arises under" the Constitution. *Romero v. International Terminal Operating Co.*, page 5, *supra*. When such a claim is brought in state court under the "saving to suitors" clause, may it be removed to the admiralty "side" of federal court, thus perhaps depriving the litigant of trial by jury? *Romero* bars removal as a "federal question," under section 1441(b). However, section 1441(a) provides that "any civil action brought in a State court of which the district courts of the United States have original jurisdiction, may be removed." An *in personam* maritime claim brought in state court is a civil action over which the federal court, sitting in admiralty, has original jurisdiction, and thus it seemingly is removable under the general language of section 1441(a), as long as the condition of section 1441(b)—that all of the defendants are nonresidents—is met. *See, e.g., Morris v. T E Marine Corp.* (5th Cir.2003). There are strong arguments to the contrary, however. One is that the "saving to suitors" clause is an express provision by Congress against such removal; this argument finds support in the dictum in *Romero* that permitting such removal would destroy the historic option that the "saving to suitors" clause gives to maritime claimants to pursue their claims in either state or federal court.

One maritime removal problem arises out of the jurisprudence holding that a 905(b) claim does not produce federal question jurisdiction. *See* Chapter XIII, *supra*. Thus in those cases in which the injured worker's duties place him on the borderline between seaman status and LHWCA coverage, the defendant's right to remove depends upon the worker's status. Because a Jones Act claim is not removable, a plaintiff seeking to avoid federal court may allege a frivolous seaman's claim and an alternative 905(b) claim. Courts generally avoid a determination of the worker's status upon trial of the motion to remand by imposing upon the defendant a heavy burden of proving that the Jones Act claim is frivolous.

If a maritime claim brought in state court is removable under 28 U.S.C.A. § 1441(a), it may lose removability when it is joined in that court with a claim which is not removable. Section 1441(c) permits removal of a removable claim which is joined with a nonremovable claim only if the claims are "separate and independent," a criterion not usually met when an unseaworthiness claim is joined with a Jones Act claim.

G.   JOINDER AND SUPPLEMENTAL JURISDICTION

The federal rules of initial joinder (joinder of claims under Fed.Civ.Proc. Rule 18, 28 U.S.C.A., and joinder of parties under Fed.Civ.Proc. Rule 20) and subsequent joinder (counterclaims and cross claims under Fed.Civ.Proc. Rule 13, third party actions under Fed.Civ.Proc. Rule 14, and intervention under Fed.Civ.Proc. Rule 24,) apply in an action in a federal court in which jurisdiction is premised upon the admiralty power. Where the Federal Rules of Civil Procedure permitted joinder of a claim over which a federal court had subject matter jurisdiction with a claim over which it did not have such jurisdiction, the federal courts developed the theory of "ancillary jurisdiction" or "pendent jurisdiction," under which a federal court sometimes would exercise jurisdiction over the nonfederal claim. In such cases, the court's jurisdiction over the state law claim was said to be an "ancillary" to the federal claim. Congress' creation of supplemental jurisdiction, 28 U.S.C.A. § 1367, continues the concepts of ancillary and pendent jurisdiction in maritime law. *See, e.g., Jerome B. Grubart, Inc. v. Great Lakes Dredge & Dock Company*, page 40, *supra*. Under *Grubart* , a tort claim which ordinarily would not be maritime may be so connected with a maritime claim that it will also be deemed a maritime tort. Thus damage-causing conduct which otherwise would be evaluated under state tort principles may arise out of or coalesce with maritime tort conduct and thus could be pursued in federal court either as a maritime tort under 28 U.S.C.A. § 1333 or as a state tort claim over which the federal court hearing the maritime claim could exercise supplemental jurisdiction.

Supplemental jurisdiction poses an additional problem in a maritime setting. When jurisdiction in a federal court is premised solely upon the admiralty power, the parties are not entitled to trial by jury. If a party to a maritime claim brought as an admiralty claim is permitted to "pend" a nonfederal (state law) cause of action, the whole case presumably will be tried in federal court without a jury. However, since the "pended" or nonfederal claim arises out of state law, the litigants usually would have been entitled to try the claim to a jury in state court. Thus application of supplemental jurisdiction in a federal court sitting in admiralty could deprive a litigant of the trial by jury to which he otherwise was entitled.

The expansive interpretation of the supplemental jurisdiction statute provided by the Supreme Court may impact upon the jurisprudential difficulties between maritime and supplemental jurisdiction. *Ortega v. Star–Kist Foods, Inc.* (S.Ct.2005).

Res judicata probably will not apply in a maritime claim unless both parties are identical to or in privity with the parties to the prior suit. *Gulf Island–IV, Inc. v. Blue Streak–Gulf Is. Ops.* (5th Cir.1994). Courts also may apply "judicial estoppel," i.e., a party is estopped from changing positions in a case to gain an unfair advantage over an opponent where the later position is clearly inconsistent with the earlier position and the first tribunal accepted and relied upon the prior inconsistent position. *New Hampshire v. Maine* (S.Ct.2001).

H. APPEALS

A final judgment in a suit brought as an admiralty claim in federal court is reviewable in the same fashion as judgments in other cases. 28 U.S.C.A. § 1291. The standard for review on appeal is that provided for all bench trials by Fed.Civ.Proc. Rule 52(a): "Findings of fact shall not be set aside unless clearly erroneous, and due regard shall be given to the opportunity of the trial court to judge ... the credibility of the witnesses."

An interlocutory judgment of a federal court sitting in admiralty may be reviewed under Rule 54(b), which permits the trial court to convert into a final judgment an order disposing of all of the claims of one party in a multiparty suit, or an order disposing of one of several claims between the same parties. Another method of review of such judgments is through certification by the district court that the decision involves a "controlling" question of law or fact under the provisions of 28 U.S.C.A. § 1292(b). In addition, 28 U.S.C.A. § 1292(a)(3), a special provision for admiralty cases, provides appeal of "[i]nterlocutory decrees of ... district courts ... determining the rights and liabilities of the parties to admiralty cases in which appeals from final decrees are allowed." The purpose of the provision is to continue the traditional admiralty practice of separate trial and appeal on the issue of liability, with subsequent trial of the damage issue before a commissioner. However, some courts have given the provision broader application.

Some states apply their own appellate standards in reviewing appeals in maritime matters. This practice arguably is acceptable in "saving to suitors" cases, but not in review of Jones Act jury trials, since the right to a jury verdict is an integral part of the seaman's substantive rights under the act, and the weight of the jury's verdict should not be diminished by a state appellate review standard.

I. REMEDIES

The struggle between the English law and equity courts and that struggle's impact upon admiralty has been recounted earlier in this chapter and in Chapter I. One of the outgrowths of the struggle was the rule that maritime courts could not grant equitable relief. This limitation developed in American maritime law into a rule that a federal court sitting in admiralty lacked "jurisdiction" over equitable matters, with the result that such a court could not grant injunctions or specific performance, enforce a trust, reform a contract because of fraud or error, or entertain an action for an accounting or an action based on an equitable title or an equitable right.

The rule was not without detractors or exceptions. One exception was that an admiralty court could entertain an equitable defense to a maritime claim. By 1966 it was clear that there were other exceptions, although the boundaries of admiralty's permissive intrusion into traditional equity matters were far from clear. Two Supreme Court cases merit special attention. In *Swift & Co. Packers v. Compania Colombiana Del Caribe, S.A.* (S.Ct.1950), the plaintiff seized a vessel allegedly owned by one defendant; a second defendant sought to vacate the attachment on the grounds that it had acquired the vessel from the first defendant prior to the seizure. When the plaintiff then sought to set aside the transfer as fraudulent, the district court concluded that it was without jurisdiction to inquire into sale of the vessel, since reformation of contracts for fraud was an equitable remedy. Reversing, the Supreme Court observed:

> Unquestionably a court of admiralty will not enforce an independent equitable claim merely because it pertains to maritime property.... But that is not the case before us. Libellants went into admiralty on a claim arising upon a contract of affreightment supplemented by charges of negligence in the nondelivery of a sea cargo—matters obviously within the admiralty jurisdiction. As an incident to that claim, in order to secure respondents' appearance and to insure the fruits of a decree in libellants' favor, they made an attachment.... *The issue of fraud arises in connection with the attachment as a means of effectuating a claim incontestably in admiralty.* To deny an admiralty court jurisdiction over this *subsidiary or derivative issue in a litigation clearly maritime* would require an absolute rule that admiralty is rigorously excluded from all contact with nonmaritime transactions and from all equitable relief, even though such nonmaritime transactions come

into play, and such equitable relief is sought, in the course of admiralty's exercise of its jurisdiction over a matter exclusively maritime. (Emphasis added).

More significant to the issue of the demise of the rule is the Court's decision in *Archawski v. Hanioti* (S.Ct.1956), in which it upheld admiralty jurisdiction over a suit for restitution. Recognizing that the issue was "to prevent unjust enrichment from a maritime contract," the Court observed that "so long as the claim asserted arises out of a maritime contract, the admiralty court has jurisdiction over it."

Archawski may have heralded the end of the concept that admiralty courts do not have the power to grant equitable remedies. It also is arguable that the concept did not survive the unification of law and admiralty rules in 1966. That unification extended federal rules pertaining to injunction and other equitable remedies to courts sitting in admiralty. The view that unification cured any lack of equity powers by admiralty courts was artfully expressed by Judge Brown of the Fifth Circuit in these words:

> The Chancellor is no longer fixed to the woolsack. He may stride the quarterdeck of maritime jurisprudence and, in the role of admiralty judge, dispense, as would his landlocked brother, that which equity and good conscience impels.

Compania Anonima Venezolana De Nav. v. Perez Export Co. (5th Cir.1962).

However, the limitation on the power of a court sitting "in admiralty" to grant equitable remedies traditionally has been phrased in terms of "jurisdiction," and Rule 82 provides that the federal rules "shall not be construed to extend ... the jurisdiction of the United States district courts." Thus it is not clear that unification has removed all limitations on equitable remedies in maritime law.

Through the admiralty power, a federal court may adjudicate claims to the ownership or possession of vessels, cargo and other maritime property. Supplemental Rules for Certain Admiralty and Maritime Claims, Fed.Civ.Proc. Rule D. A petitory action is one in which title to the property is adjudicated independently of possession. The traditional rule is that the plaintiff in the petitory action must assert legal title to the vessel or other property, and not merely an equitable interest. The possessory action is one in which the right to possess the vessel or other property is at issue.

Prior to 1954, there was doubt whether a federal court sitting in admiralty had jurisdiction to partition a vessel. In addition, the admiralty substantive rule was that a court which had jurisdiction could not partition a vessel unless the parties in disagreement were the owners of equal shares. If the owners of unequal shares disagreed about the use of the vessel, the decision of the majority owners prevailed, but the minority owners could require a bond to secure the return of the vessel from any voyage undertaken without their consent. In *Madruga v. Superior Court* (S.Ct.1954), the Supreme

Court ruled that under the "saving to suitors" clause of 28 U.S.C.A. § 1333, federal and state courts have concurrent jurisdiction to order the partition of ships in a proceeding *in personam,* and that there is no federal admiralty rule barring judicial partition of a vessel unless the ownership interests are deadlocked. Accordingly, Supplemental Rule D, Admiralty and Maritime Claims, provides for partition actions as well as petitory and possessory actions.

The Federal Arbitration Act makes any written provision in a maritime transaction valid and enforceable except for "such grounds as exist at law or in equity for the revocation of any contract." 9 U.S.C.A. § 2. A seaman's employment contract is exempted from the application of the FAA (9 U.S.C. Sec. 1).

The American courts generally uphold agreements to submit to foreign arbitration. *Vimar Seguros y Reaseguros, S.A. v. M/V Sky Reefer* (S.Ct. 1995). Foreign awards are enforced through the 1958 Convention on the Recognition and Enforcement to Foreign Arbitral Awards, which the United States has ratified.

*

INDEX

References are to Pages

399

†